MAJOR ACCOUNT SALES STRATEGIES

Breaking the
SIX-FIGURE BARRIER
in Consultive Selling

MAJOR ACCOUNT SALES STRATEGIES

Breaking the
SIX-FIGURE BARRIER
in Consultive Selling

ALAN SHIFFLETT

S$_L^t$

St. Lucie Press

Boca Raton London New York Washington, D.C.

Library of Congress Cataloging-in-Publication Data

Shifflett, Alan L.
    Major account sales strategies : an easy-to-use guide to winning large
sales / Alan L. Shifflett.
        p. cm.
    Originally published: Consultative sales strategies / Alan L. Shifflett.
    ISBN 1-57444-288-0 (alk. paper)
    1. Selling. 2. Sales management. I. Shifflett, Alan L. Consultative sales strategies.
II. Title.
HF5438.25 .S483 2000
658.8′1—dc21   00-039042
                                                    CIP

© 2000 by CRC Press LLC
St. Lucie Press is an imprint of CRC Press LLC

No claim to original U.S. Government works
International Standard Book Number 1-57444-288-0
Library of Congress Card Number 00-039042
Printed in the United States of America 1 2 3 4 5 6 7 8 9 0
Printed on acid-free paper

PREFACE

Major Account Sales Strategies, first written in the late eighties, is the result of two decades of research involving the study of hundreds of successful (and unsuccessful) salespeople who sell in the major account arena.

The original version has since been totally revised, because over the past decade the purchasing dynamics of large organizations have become quite complex and buyers vastly more sophisticated. As a result, many of the established sales techniques that were accepted as the standard even a few years ago are now only marginally effective.

In order to be successful in today's business environment, the top performers have become consultants, employing highly professional tools and strategies to help their clients accomplish goals such as becoming more efficient or reducing operating expenses. They spent years of trial and error to learn the best ways to win major corporate contracts, but you don't have to. You can shave years off of your learning curve by using the tools and techniques covered in *Major Account Sales Strategies.*

You will be able to significantly increase your income immediately as you become more effective at selling applied solutions to major corporations. You will also be able to grow your established accounts a lot faster. You will learn how to develop long-term relationships with your clients by using a consultative approach that will lead to better problem solving, and increased benefits for your customer.

By investing the time and effort necessary to understand and satisfy the needs, concerns, and desires of your prospects and clients, you will represent an invaluable resource to them. In essence, you will be partnering with them. Your contribution will lead to creative solutions to improve the organization's efficiency and profitability, which will help your contact in the organization win bigger bonuses and raises, as well as faster promotions.

In fact, once you master the consultative approach, you will have to turn down business because today's sophisticated decision-makers are looking for sales professionals like you who will actively support their customers, not just drop the product on their desk.

The book is literally packed with great tips, and many readers have indicated that they learned something new every time they referred to different sections. In fact, you could double, or even triple your income as you learn how to:

- ❏ Target the best prospects in your territory
- ❏ Spend more quality time with qualified prospects
- ❏ Improve contact management
- ❏ Conduct comprehensive investigations

- ❏ Identify each layer of the buying chain
- ❏ Sell solutions instead of price
- ❏ Develop consultative sales strategies
- ❏ Coordinate your action plan with the prospect's buying cycle
- ❏ Customize your proposals
- ❏ Deliver dynamic presentations
- ❏ Effect a smooth account implementation
- ❏ Strategically manage and grow your account base

**ALL OF THIS WILL LEAD TO HIGHER COMMISSIONS
AND FASTER CAREER GROWTH
AS YOU TOTALLY OUTCLASS YOUR COMPETITORS!**

*   *   *

THE AUTHOR

Alan Shifflett is President of Corporate Training Specialists, a nationwide sales training firm, and co-founder of the Association of Paging Resellers. In addition to earning a BS degree in business administration from Towson State University, he has had extensive sales and management training at such renowned organizations as Motorola, BellSouth, and Learning International.

Mr. Shifflett has over two decades of successful corporate sales and management experience in the telecommunications industry, and he is certified as a trainer by Learning International, Business Efficacy, MobileComm, and American Paging.

Having designed training seminars and workshops for a variety of organizations, from small entrepreneurial ventures to Fortune 500 corporations, Mr. Shifflett brings a realistic perspective to the training arena. He provides salespeople with the skills and tools necessary to compete effectively in a rapidly changing business environment; he teaches them a consultative approach that leads to better problem solving, and results in long-term relationships with their clients.

CONTENTS

CHAPTER ONE

Rules of Engagement

"While winning a major contract can be a serious rush, the sales process itself is usually a serious pain. I have often wondered if large organizations send their buyers to special courses that teach creative ways to torture salespeople."

CHAPTER 1: Rules of Engagement

TOPIC 1.1: The Major Account Arena

SKILLSET TOPIC(S)
- ❑ **Organizational purchasing dynamics**
- ❑ **Buying cycle coordination**

OBJECTIVE

To review the impact of the purchasing process of large organizations as it relates to your strategy, action plan, and coordinating the steps of the sale.

BENEFITS

- ✓ Isolate corporate purchasing patterns.
- ✓ Improve sales strategies and plans.
- ✓ Lower the stress on your prospects (and yourself) when you conform to their buying cycle.

> *"It has been my experience that more large sales are lost because of poor strategy, than as a result of pricing issues."*

You have probably noticed that in most cases closing small accounts is relatively easy, unlike the really large contracts, which are usually significantly harder to win. It's not just a figment of your imagination.

Large organizations typically have much more complicated purchasing procedures than small ones, so it takes an entirely different set of skills to be consistently successful in that arena.

The intricate purchasing procedures that are typical for most large companies are partly the result of the new layers of support staff, management, and departments that organizations tend to add as they staff up to accommodate expansion.

In addition, the more money a public company spends on goods and services, the tighter its checks and balances. This makes the selling process more difficult, and often causes the buying process to drag out even longer than normal. If and when the company becomes involved in a major restructuring, it can make the delay a lot worse, especially since it is usually totally unexpected.

At this point you might be thinking that most of the major accounts you have worked on have had fairly short buying cycles. That was probably because those particular companies happened to be shopping for a new vendor when you met them, which will change when you start specifically targeting major organizations. You will often initiate the sales process, not come in at the end, so the sale will sometimes take months to complete. Even when you catch a company near the end of its contract, if conditions change, the sale will sometimes still take longer than you expected to close.

While the steps to make a small sale might sometimes happen in one sales call, that process will typically take longer with a large company, even when there are no unexpected delays. The individual steps usually become a lot more critical in developing a successful sales strategy.

It is my experience that more large sales are lost because of poor strategy than because of pricing issues. Less experienced salespeople typically make a good proposal, but have no plan as to what they will do if that company does not make a decision within a short period of time. As a result, if the decision is delayed their enthusiasm fades, and they sometimes stop calling. By the time the bid is finally awarded they are already off on a new adventure, so the sale is lost. Even worse, they may lose a few smaller sales when they stop working on them because they expect to quickly win the large one.

Tables 1.1 through 1.3 provide a snapshot that shows how the sales process is typically affected by the size of the organization and its buying pattern.

In most cases there are few obstacles when you deal with smaller companies. This type of prospect is usually easy to win or lose; the action is fast, and you know where you are in a very short period of time. You might describe that type of prospect as:

The "QUICKIE"

TYPICAL PROFILE
- ➤ **Account size:** small
- ➤ **Buying cycle:** immediate - 30 days
- ➤ **Sales process:** fast, typically 1 - 3 sales calls

DEFINITION
- ❑ They are not under contract/contract expires soon.
- ❑ If a nonuser, they are funded for your product/service.
- ❑ You often present to ultimate decision-maker.
- ❑ Your contact has the authority to make the purchase.

COMPATIBILITY CHECKLIST
- ✓ They are unhappy with their vendor.
- ✓ Your timing is perfect/they are actively looking.
- ✓ The chemistry between you and the owner is good.
- ✓ Your service represents the perfect solution to their needs.
- ✓ You have a technological edge or are competitively priced.

Table 1.1

The purchasing dynamics of medium-sized companies tend to make the sale a bit more difficult, which also translates into more time spent on the courtship. They might even be in love with their current salesperson, in which case you have to be patient until they start being taken for granted. You could call this type of prospect:

"CURRENTLY COMMITTED"

TYPICAL PROFILE
> **Account size:** medium-sized to large
> **Buying cycle:** 30 - 90 days
> **Sales process:** 2 - 4 sales calls

DEFINITION
- Might start with a request for a proposal to evaluate their vendor.
- It might be a nonuser that is investigating alternatives.
- You may be dealing with a recommender or influencer.
- The decision might require an out-of-state approval.
- Often takes a while to win since it is probably not a top priority for the decision-maker(s).
- Requires a comprehensive sales strategy.
- Their needs may require that your product/service be modified.

COMPATIBILITY CHECKLIST
- ✓ They might be happy with their vendor.
- ✓ You might have a reasonable technological edge for your product/service.
- ✓ The decision is typically more impersonal.
- ✓ You might have a slight pricing advantage.

Table 1.2

The largest companies will often be very loyal to their account manager. They are usually not motivated to make a change unless there is substantial justification because, at their size, change can be very disruptive. In general, they will present you with an even more challenging set of conditions. As you can see from the brief description that follows, large companies have a built-in defense system that is often tough to bridge:

"HARD TO GET"

TYPICAL PROFILE
> **Account size:** very large
> **Buying cycle:** 90 - 360 days
> **Sales process:** 4 - 10+ sales calls

DEFINITION
❑ Often initiated as a result of your prospecting activities.
❑ Might be a nonuser who has not recognized a need for your service.
❑ You may start out dealing with a screener, like an office manager.
❑ You may be allowed to consult on the development of a bid.
❑ You may not yet have the technical ability to deliver.
❑ Prospect may go through major change, like an acquisition or merger.
❑ May assign a low priority to your project/feel it is too much work.
❑ Decision-maker may change due to promotion/transfer/termination.

COMPATIBILITY CHECKLIST
✓ They might be delighted with/loyal to their current vendor.
✓ You might be higher priced.
✓ The decision is typically made by spreadsheet analysis.
✓ You will typically have to bond with multiple parties.

Table 1.3

Table 1.4 compares the different scenarios that we have just reviewed, making the challenges of selling to large companies quite clear:

COMPARATIVE SALES CONDITIONS

VARIABLES	SIZE		
	SMALL	**MEDIUM**	**LARGE**
CONTACT	Decision-maker	Influencer	Recommender
PRESENTATION	Easy	Fairly easy	Complex
NEEDS	Simple	Fairly Involved	Complicated
VULNERABILITY	High	Moderate	Low
COMPETITION	Moderate	Challenging	Cut-throat
EVALUATION	Emotional	Mixed	Spreadsheet
CONTROL	High	Variable	Low
SALES CYCLE	1 - 6 weeks	2 - 24 weeks	4 - 52 weeks
GROWTH	Slow	Variable	Fast
MAINTENANCE	Very little	Moderate	Difficult

Table 1.4

As a result of the complexity of the buying process, companies often assign salespeople who are mature, experienced, well-educated professionals to sell to major accounts and government agencies. In order to be successful selling against them, you have to consult with your prospects, provide creative solutions to their problems, develop a good sales strategy, and plan how you will overcome any obstacles that you might encounter. This is demonstrated in Figure 1.5.

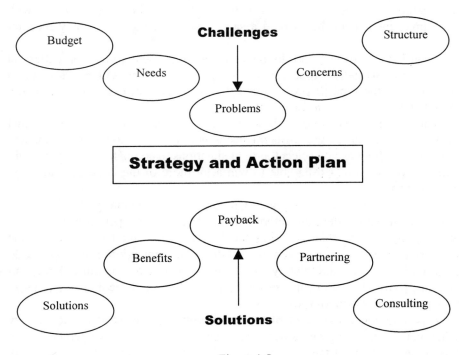

Figure 1.5

Since selling to large organizations can take months, and it is extremely competitive, you need to keep working the smaller accounts, regardless of how good you become, until you have a lot of very hot prospects in the hopper. That way, if you win a major account it is like a bonus; but, if you lose it, you can still pay the rent.

When a sale you have been working on takes longer than expected to close, you have to adjust to their buying cycle rather than try to push because it is usually out of the control of your contact. With very little work, the letters and tools in the Case Study sections will enable you to keep in touch with your contact when their buying cycle stretches out, expectedly or unexpectedly.

While a long sales cycle can be frustrating, there are some advantages. To begin with, if you get lucky, you might not even have to compete with their current vendor; if the salesperson who is handling the account gets a new job before the prospect makes a decision, you will win by default.

When you are competing with multiple vendors, a longer selling period will enable your contact to become totally comfortable with you by the time they do make a decision. That will give you an edge against any competitor who entered the process after you did. As long as you use professional sales tools and techniques, your prospect will naturally be more likely to trust you with their investment than they would a salesperson that they have only recently met.

Even if the prospect had doubts or reservations when you first called on them, the consultative approach we are going to cover will prove to them that you are the type of professional they can rely on, especially after you have been courting them for months.

You can improve your odds even more if you develop a strategy that provides solutions for the different needs and wants of the decision-makers involved. As long as you select the right situations to compete for, and the right strategy to use, you will be able to win a lot more of the large accounts you make proposals to.

But that is only the beginning. Once you win the account, you will be able to earn even more orders and referrals if you become an expert at helping them avoid problems, especially during the honeymoon. You have to make the delivery painless, minimize the time lost during the transition, and keep a good record of their account history. That record can later be turned into an account profile that you can use for future analysis and recommendations as they grow and as technology changes.

This may sound like a lot of work, but you really can't afford to be lazy when you are pursuing major accounts. Usually, only about five percent of the businesses in a given territory would qualify as being very large, and at any given point in time only a small percentage of them will be vulnerable. Besides, losing a major contract will cost you a very large commission and give your competition control of that account, perhaps for years afterwards.

The bottom line is that if you want to win a high percentage of the significant opportunities that you work on, you have to be willing to spend quality time on each one, not just rush through them. That translates into the serious courtship of a major account instead of the "love them and leave them" tactics you might use with smaller sales.

That should not be too difficult because the sales process happens to be very similar to courtship, although nowhere near as much fun. I can almost see that skeptical look on your face, but I think Figure 1.6 will help change your mind.

RITUALS

Sales	*Courtship*
Target prospects	*Flirt*
Create an interest	*The pick-up*
Add to database	*Add to black book*
Meet and qualify	*First date*
Identify need/desires	*Check compatibility*
Propose	*Pop the question*
Negotiate terms	*Engagement*
Delivery	*The wedding*
Take care of problems	*The honeymoon*
Grow the account	*Family planning*
Block competitors	*Keep the flame alive*

Figure 1.6

It has been suggested that I thought of the comparison illustrated in Figure 1.6 because I was romantically deprived in my formative years, but I would prefer to think that it was just too obvious to miss. For instance, think about the last really easy sale that you made. Wasn't it kind of like love at first sight?

In fact, you are probably working with at least one prospect right now that is unfaithful (talking to other salespeople), and I am willing to bet that a few customers are guilty of bigamy (using multiple vendors). And is waiting for a prospect's contract to expire really any different than waiting for someone's divorce to become final?

Of course, there are also some significant differences between sales and romance, the most important being the fact that you will never inherit in-laws after you win the sale, which is a good thing.

*   *   *

Study Guide

This course is comprised of six different components. There are five sections in the book and the disk, and all of them are integrated to provide a practical applied learning experience.

Two of the sections in the book, the Exercises and the Case Study, are designed to give you a chance to practice using the tools and concepts before you try them out on your unsuspecting customers and prospects. A third section, Assignments, will help you apply those tools to sales that you are currently working on.

When there are exercises and/or assignments for you to complete, there are examples of the questions or application at the end of the topic, along with reference to the specific file location on the disk where you can respond. Make sure that you save the original file of any documents or forms that you want to reuse per the instructions in the tutorial located in the Appendix (Exhibit C, Page 271).

A basic description of each section follows:

1. **Topics:**
    Each topic covers tips, tools, and techniques for a specific phase of the sales process, with illustrations and practical examples that demonstrate how they would work when you apply them.

2. **Case Study:**
    There are actually two different scenarios in the case study. The first scenario provides you with a step-by-step example of how the different tools affect a particular aspect of the sales process. The second scenario provides you the opportunity to practice developing a strategy, an action plan, and an ROI Analysis.

3. **Exercises:**
    Each exercise is a review of the key concepts in the preceding topic. You can answer the questions in the Exercise Folder on your disk, and then check the answer key in the Appendix to verify your responses.

4. **Assignments:**
    This section provides you with an opportunity to actually apply the tools

and concepts to your own prospects and customers at every stage of the sales process. There are no answer keys in the Appendix, but they will be easy to complete after you read the related topic. Again, all of the appropriate forms that you need can be found in the Assignment Folder on your disk. Simple instructions can be found on page 271.

5. **Appendix:**
   Contains several reference exhibits, such as a detailed description of various research sources, a tutorial on how to use the disc, and the answer key for the exercises and case study applications.

6. **Disk:**
   Contains folders with files for each exercise, assignment, and case study, as well as samples of correspondence, the proposal, and a variety of account management tools that you can customize as needed.

*   *   *

TOPIC 1.1: Exercise

1. Fill in the purchasing dynamics that you might face in each of the areas listed below:

VARIABLES	SIZE	
	SMALL	LARGE
Contact		
Vulnerability		
Competition		
Evaluation		
Sales Cycle		

2. List some of the reasons why large organizations are often difficult to sell to.

_____

_____

_____

_____

_____

_____

_____

Answer Key: Page 264
Disk: Exercise Folder.

CHAPTER TWO

High-Impact Prospecting

> *"You really don't HAVE to use an effective prospecting strategy to find major accounts, because if you talk to enough people you are bound to eventually find some. After all, even blind squirrels find an occasional acorn now and then (although fat blind squirrels are fairly rare)."*

CHAPTER 2: High-Impact Prospecting

TOPIC 2.1: Target Selection

SKILLSET TOPIC(S)
- ❑ Developing a prime prospect profile
- ❑ Targeting traditional major user groups
- ❑ Identifying alternate vertical market(s)

OBJECTIVE
To help you target organizations with the potential to use a large volume of your product/services, including all of the organization's related departments, divisions, and locations within your territory.

BENEFITS
- ✓ Spend more time on qualified prospects.
- ✓ Develop industry-specific knowledge and skills.
- ✓ Generate higher average revenue per account.
- ✓ Manage a smaller number of accounts.
- ✓ Improve account growth potential.
- ✓ Get referrals to other major users.

> *"Research is time consuming, but either you spend a little time in advance to find qualified prospects, or a lot of time on situations that are less productive."*

I'm sure you would agree that looking for the perfect prospect is a lot easier than looking for the perfect mate. After all, there are probably very few attractive millionaires who are single, sane, and totally compatible with you.

But as you have probably noticed, random prospecting rarely seems to turn up a high percentage of those perfect prospects. The truth is, if you plan to make serious money your time is too valuable to spend strictly on random prospecting; you need to work smart.

Fortunately, there is a proven method for finding prime sales prospects who are major users of your product/service, and it is a relatively easy system to use. There are three basic steps involved. All you have to do is:

STEP #1: Research your existing clients to identify high-end users and develop a target list.

In order to analyze your customers, you would begin by listing your top 20 customers in order by size on a four-column sheet (refer to Appendix Exhibit A), and then list their Standard Industry Classification code. I would also suggest you list any related/sub industries.

The Standard Industry Coding (SIC) system that the government uses to classify businesses is extremely easy to use. A copy of the directory is included on disk along with hundreds of different classifications that you can use to identify specific types of companies, as we will discuss in a moment.

If you are unfamiliar with SIC codes, the system basically works as follows:

There are four basic categories:
a) Manufacturing
b) Government
c) Wholesale
d) Retail/Direct.

All businesses fall somewhere within those groups, and they are coded as follows:
2-digit = Industry
4-digit = Sub-Category
6-digit = Specific Classification

EXAMPLE:

15	Building Construction – General Contractors
1521	General Contractors – Single Family Homes
152101	Patio and Deck Builders

Reviewing your customer base will provide a wealth of valuable information, including who the top-end users of your product/service are. Similar companies will probably also be major users/prospects, so you obviously want to focus on them, which you can do once you develop a list of industries to target.

Once you complete a customer analysis, your list might look like Table 2.1.1, which represents a typical list of organizations that would contain good prospects for most products/services.

Target Industry Sectors

GOVERNMENT	INSTITUTIONAL	PRIVATE INDUSTRY
Federal Agencies	Universities	Fortune 1000 Companies
State Agencies	Colleges	Hospitals
Local Agencies	Schools	Financial Institutions
	Public Utilities	

Table 2.1.1

STEP #2: Get lists of companies with the same SIC as your top customers.

In addition to targeting prospects by SIC, you can be even more effective if you focus your search further by using any additional information that you learn about your major customers, such as how many employees they have. Make sure that you take multiple locations into account as part of your analysis.

Information about other companies in your territory can be found in several places. The Internet is a great source, but there are also a variety of databases that you might want to consider if your company does not already subscribe to them, such as The American Business List (which is on CD at most public libraries).

There are also excellent reference manuals such as *The Dunn & Bradstreet Million Dollar Directory*, which is available at your local library. Each source will provide different information, such the number of employees a particular company has, how much their sales are, and/or things such the names of the officers of the organization. We will discuss sources in the next section, and there is a detailed description of the various sources available to you in the Appendix.

STEP #3: The third step is a little more difficult, but well worth the effort, because it can really give an edge over your competition. You want to do some research to find other vertical markets with unidentified needs that do not use your product/service, and/or industries that use an alternative product or service that you could improve on. In other words, you want to find other business groups that do not use your product or service, either because they are unaware of the potential benefits, or because they are using an alternative solution that is less efficient or more expensive.

Since these companies have a need in areas that you could improve by getting them to use your product/service, they would represent optimum prospects. And if your competitors have not yet found that application, you don't have to fight off a pack of hungry wolves.

As an example, you might think that recruiters are not really a good prospect for paging because they are in the office all day. They are, in fact, potential prospects because candidates and employers often have to contact them after business hours.

Once you have completed these steps, your target list will be much more specific. For instance, if you sold paging solutions to the business community, your target market list would represent the largest paging user groups in industries where people work outside the office and need to keep in touch. A list of major paging users by industry would typically have the cast of characters listed in Table 2.1.2.

Paging Target List

SIC Code	User Group
48	COMMUNICATIONS SERVICES
91	GOVERNMENT SERVICES
73	MISC. BUSINESS SERVICES
42	TRUCKING
80	HEALTH and ALLIED SERVICES
73	COMPUTER and DATA PROC.
40	RAILROAD TRANSPORTATION.
50	ELECTRICAL GOODS
15	RESIDENTIAL BUILDING CONST.

Table 2.1.2

The research itself is not difficult, just time consuming, but it will be time well spent. Even the best prospector in the world will do poorly if they waste too much time on relatively small prospects and have too few large prospects in the pipeline.

Doing your homework will enable you to avoid chasing phantom opportunities, so the question is whether you want to spend a little time in advance to find qualified prospects, or a lot of time on situations that are less productive.

*　　*　　*

TOPIC 2.1: Case Study

The tools and strategies we are going to cover in this text are tried and tested, having worked for salespeople who sell a variety of products and services. I am confident they will work just as well for you.

Whether you sell a very high-ticket product or service, like large computer networks, or a smaller ticket item such as copiers or a long distance service, you need to use professional tools and an effective strategy similar to those used in the case study.

I had originally considered using a "widget" to demonstrate the concepts and tools that we are going to cover, but I wanted you to be able to easily apply the examples to your sales process, and "widgets" wouldn't really do the trick. After evaluating several different products and services, looking for something that would involve elements that are common to most products/services, I finally decided that paging comes closest to fitting the bill for the following reasons:

❑ Paging products are both tangible (the beeper), and intangible (the service).
❑ The customer can be a small company, or among the largest companies in the world.
❑ It could be a one-shot sale, or the account could grow larger each year.
❑ The account might never need service, or it might require constant maintenance.
❑ The equipment can be either sold or leased.
❑ The sales process can be as short as 15 minutes, or as long as three years.
❑ It can be low-tech, or require a consultative approach demanding a very sophisticated understanding of wireless technology and business applications. An example is two-way paging, where two or more people can use their pagers to directly transmit and receive complex text messages in the field.
❑ The sale can be simple, or can require more sophisticated tools such as Return on Investment calculations for cost justification.
❑ The benefits are both tangible, and intangible. For instance, paging typically costs substantially less to use than comparable cellular fees, which is a tangible benefit. A two-way pager can substitute for a laptop when no telephone line is available, creating a file of messages received that you can download to your computer, or store for future reference. That is clearly an intangible benefit.

Now let's get on with the show. Assume that you represent TrueBeep, a nationwide paging carrier, and you have just completed your target SIC list. High-tech organizations that provide consulting services are in the top category, so they become your primary targets. You decide to also pursue associations, because your territory includes Washington, DC, which is where most of the associations have their headquarters.

Armed with that information, you start doing research on the Internet, where you find that there are several major organizations in your territory that fit the bill in both categories. There are a lot of possibilities when you study the high-tech companies on your list, but a company called NetCom catches your eye. You recently read an article about them in the business section of the newspaper, so you decide to start there.

Scenario #1

Prospect: NetCom

Background

NetCom is an international company providing systems and software engineering. They have 15,000 employees, 8,000 of which are in the US. They have different teams that work in the field, such as consultants, project managers, installation teams, trainers, service technicians, and programmers.

Of all the associations on your list, the first prospect you target is:

Scenario #2

Prospect: Association of the Romantically Deprived (not affiliated with the Association of the Romantically Depraved).

Background
ARD is a national association with millions of members. You targeted them because, in addition to selling your service to the various departments, they will usually let vendors set up membership discount programs, which could lead to a lot of repeat business.

Now that we have targeted some prospects, let's review some of the potential techniques you can use to get an appointment.

*   *   *

P.S. I believe that all of the names of individuals and companies used in this book are figments of my imagination; but, if any party or organization I use in my examples really exists, I apologize in advance.

TOPIC 2.1: Exercise

❑ List the primary vertical market that you target, and the qualities that you look for in a qualified major account:

PRIMARY VERTICAL MARKET

Industry:
_____

Criteria:
_____

_____

_____

_____

_____

_____

_____

_____

_____

Appendix: Page 265
Disk: Exercise Folder

TOPIC 2.1: Assignment

1. List your top clients by account volume/growth pattern, and identify their industry/SIC. You should fill in the last two columns after we cover the appropriate topic.

COMPANY	INDUSTRY/SIC	DEPTS/LOC	POTENTIAL

2. Develop a target list of prospects that you want to pursue who are in the same industries as your largest clients. Skip the last column for now.

COMPANY	CONTACT(S)	PHONE #	DEPTS/LOC

Disk: Application Folder

CHAPTER 2: High-Impact Prospecting

TOPIC 2.2: Prospecting Strategies

SKILLSET TOPIC(S)
- ❑ **Using a combined marketing approach**
- ❑ **Lead sources**
- ❑ **Analyzing your territory**

OBJECTIVE

Discuss strategies for finding organizations that fit your major account profile, and a method for organizing your prospecting activities to maximize your effectiveness.

BENEFITS
- ✓ Develop new lead sources.
- ✓ Improve lead source utilization.
- ✓ Decrease wasted time with better time and territory management.
- ✓ Spend more time on viable prospects.

> *"Shotgun Marketing does offer some distinct advantages, because even though they might not be the very largest organizations in your territory, you will always find some prospects to sell to."*

When you think about it, prospecting is exactly the same as looking for love, including the fact that in both cases we typically look in all the wrong places.

That was basically true about my marketing technique before I learned how to target qualified prospects. My strategy was simple. I basically lusted after any suspect that had a pulse, a process that could best be described as "shotgun marketing". If this sounds like the approach that you use, you probably run into more small companies than large ones.

While the shotgun approach may not be the best system for finding major accounts, it actually does offer some distinct advantages over the targeted approach that we will soon discuss. To begin with, it is an easy system to use, since all you have to do is get out of your car and knock on doors. Although they might not be the largest organizations in your territory, you will always find some prospects that are willing to buy.

SHOTGUN MARKETING

DEFINITION: Randomly calling or visiting any business that could qualify for your product or service, regardless of size. Also commonly referred to as the dreaded "Cold Call." The advantages and disadvantages of this method are:

ADVANTAGE	WEAKNESS
• Excellent territory penetration • Variety of business applications • Concentrated activity pattern • More appointments/less driving • Referrals to adjoining businesses • Large quantity of prospects • Short average sales cycle • Decisions are less price-sensitive • Easier to penetrate • Less competitive • Deal directly with decision-maker	• Requires more qualifying • Less vertical market specialization • Smaller average account size • Larger customer base to manage • Referrals will typically be smaller • accounts

The shotgun approach will generally get you the type of results that follow:

TYPICAL APPOINTMENT YIELD
The shotgun approach usually yields a lower ratio of qualified leads than a targeted approach, with smaller average account size. For instance, 20 cold calls might produce the following results:

Immediate: 0 Appointments
Short-term: 1 Appointment (within 2 weeks)
Long-term: 2 Appointments (within 90 days)
Total: 3 Appointments (15% appointment ratio)

While this approach will definitely pay the bills, and you do want to continue using it until you are so popular that you are booked for a year in advance, it is not the most effective way to prospect for large accounts. To make it more efficient, you need to apply certain criteria, such as calling on the businesses around your scheduled appointments, especially when you call on major customers and prospects (large organizations tend to locate in similar environments).

Another way to increase your prospecting efficiency is to use a variety of lead sources. Depending on the type of information you get, some of those sources could be classified as shotgun sources, while others are more targeted. If a source provides information that you can use to target specific companies, like how many employees a company has, or what SIC code they fall under, it could be classified as a targeted source. On the other hand, if the information that you get is vague, such as the fact that a company is moving, it might be valuable, but should probably fall under the classification of shotgun information.

The list that follows represents the variety of sources that you can use as part of a smart shotgun approach.

SHOTGUN LEAD SOURCES

- Yellow Pages

- Fairs and Trade Shows

- Tip Clubs

- Chamber of Commerce Directories

- Trade and Professional Association Lists

- Business Magazines

- Trade Journals

- Contacts Influential Lists

- Newspapers

- Referrals

- Prospecting while Traveling

- Competitor's Reference Lists

- Lost Customers

Even though the preceding sources are obvious, you might not be utilizing all of them to their greatest potential. For more information about each source, and some practical tips, review the detailed descriptions in the Appendix (Exhibit D, Page 273). If I haven't already bored you to death, let's look at how a more targeted approach works.

TARGET MARKETING

DEFINITION: Selecting companies based on specific criteria within vertical markets that historically have a need for a large volume of your product or service, as we discussed in Target Selection. Let's look at the advantages and disadvantages of this approach:

ADVANTAGE	WEAKNESS
• Requires less qualifying	• Small window of prospects
• Large average volume orders	• More competitive market
• Fewer customers to manage	• Wider geographic distribution
• Industry specialization (you become an expert on their industry)	• Longer buying cycle
	• Hard to penetrate
• Reference selling	• Require intense maintenance
• "Birds of a Feather" referrals	• Decisions are pricing sensitive
	• Seldom deal with decision-maker

As you can see, each technique has different advantages and weaknesses, but you can leverage the strengths of each for maximum effectiveness by combining them. When you conduct research to find major opportunities, be very specific about the profile you are looking for to make the results manageable. If you use smart research criteria, you will quickly reach the point where you will be able to spend minimal time on new prospecting, yet still make top commissions.

As an example, there might be 100,000 businesses in your territory, but perhaps only 40,000 use your product/service. Without any qualifying criteria, you would have to talk to 40,000 prospects to find out which companies were the largest. If you do a good job in the research phase, like specifying companies that have more than 100 employees, that number might be reduced to 2,000. I don't know about you, but I find 2,000 prospects a lot less daunting than 40,000.

Unfortunately, that doesn't mean that you will have a ton of free time at the pool right away. The sales tools we will be covering do require a lot of work at first, but I can assure you that it is well worth the effort. In fact, they can represent the difference between your being good at what you do, and being great.

Having convinced you that doing research to target the major organizations in your territory will be worth the effort (I hope), let's look at the results you might expect from this approach:

TYPICAL APPOINTMENT YIELD

Targeted prospecting usually yields a fairly high ratio of qualified leads, with large average account size. Your results for 20 calls might look like this:

Immediate: 1 appointment (within two weeks)
Short-term: 2 appointments (within 45 days)
Long-term: 5 appointments (within 90-360 days)
Total: 8 appointments (40% appointment ratio)

TARGETED LEAD SOURCES

- The Internet

- National Business List Brokers (like American Business Lists and Dun & Bradstreet)

- *R.L. Polk & Company City Directory*

■ *Dun & Bradstreet Million Dollar Directory*

■ *Martindale Hubble Directory*

■ Manufacturer Directories

■ *American Medical Directory*

■ Alternate Library Sources (librarians are usually a fountain of knowledge)

Each territory has different characteristics that you need to take into account to decide what marketing approach will work best. If any business is a potential prospect, you should combine both approaches, whereas if the prospects in your territory are very spread out, you may have to rely more heavily on targeting to find prime prospects.

On the other hand, if most of your prospects are in business and/or industrial parks, the shotgun approach is perfect. Don't forget to prospect around your appointments, especially with your largest prospects and customers.

*   *   *

TOPIC 2.2: Exercise

1. Describe the two marketing approaches discussed in this topic.

Shotgun Marketing:

_____

_____

_____

Target Marketing:

_____

_____

_____

2. List three benefits, weaknesses, and sources for each approach:

ADVANTAGES

Shotgun   **Targeted**

_____   _____
_____   _____
_____   _____

WEAKNESSES

Shotgun   **Targeted**

_____   _____
_____   _____
_____   _____

SOURCES

Shotgun   **Targeted**

_____   _____
_____   _____
_____   _____

TOPIC 2.2: Assignment

❑ Do library/Internet research on any major prospects that you have set an appointment with, as well as those that you are working up a proposal for (use form on disk).

❑ Develop a profile for each prospect, getting key information that you can feed into the conversation to indicate that you have done your homework. Make a special note of anything that could affect your strategy, or that you may want to explore further, such as what their competitors or customers are doing (use form on disk).

❑ Pick one or two industries to concentrate on. Make notes about what you know regarding the specifics of the industry, such as trends, what type of customers they have, applications, and any industry jargon that you might be able to pick up from Web sites, etc.

CHAPTER 2: High-Impact Prospecting

TOPIC 2.3: Getting the Appointment

SKILLSET TOPIC(S)
❑ **Using a multiple contact strategy**
❑ **Defining lead types**
❑ **Prioritizing and classifying leads for follow-up**

OBJECTIVE
Review different techniques to get more appointments with qualified prospects, and effective criteria for classifying future leads for appropriate action.

BENEFITS
✓ Increase your appointment set ratio.
✓ Improve future lead follow-up procedures.

> *"In order to win more major accounts, you have to set guidelines as to which accounts to pursue, how much time to spend on them, and what type of action to take."*

Whether you are bold or shy, there is virtually no difference between the way you get a date and the way you get a sales appointment.

The "Bold" approach: stopping by to chat with the receptionist or calling them; the "Shy" approach: sending a letter, fax, or e-mail before calling. Of course, the best technique is to use both approaches at different times, just like you would if you were dating.

In fact, the perfect prospecting strategy also includes getting referrals from customers and co-workers who sell in different territories, as well as joining a lead exchange club so that you can network with salespeople who sell a different product or service. Since you are really in business for yourself in a practical sense, you could even hire someone to work from home. They could do research, call to identify the decision-maker, and even set appointments for you.

The truth is, when you start targeting major organizations you pretty much have to use a combination of approach methods because you will typically only sell a few when you first contact them (refer to Figure 1.4).

You will often get the dreaded "I'm not interested" response from employees in large companies, especially when you are talking to the wrong person. You have to keep in mind that it is a refusal by the prospect to pursue the matter, not a rejection of you as an individual. Even when you get to the right contact, they may be having a bad morning or be up to their neck in alligators, which still does not relate to you personally.

The good news is that, frequently, all is not lost in those situations, just delayed. If you keep track of them, as we will discuss later in this chapter, they will sometimes become easier to penetrate as you get more experience, or when they become dissatisfied with their vendor. Some will even become qualified prospects as your company brings new products and services to market.

Needless to say, while you want to keep track of the prospects that you can't initially penetrate, you want to avoid wasting time on leads that you can't possibly win. For instance, unless you can improve the level of service for a company that is paying far less than you would charge, you need to move on.

However, when you think that a particular prospect is qualified, but your initial attempt has been less than successful, it is time to use a different approach. Instead of continuing to call by phone and leave messages, try sending an e-mail, fax, or letter to prospects who are playing hard to get.

I have taken the liberty of classifying some of the forms of refusal that you typically experience while prospecting, and have included some suggestions as to what action, if any, you might want to take in each type of situation in Figure 2.3.1.

TEASERS

"CURRENTLY COMMITTED"

This type of prospect conforms to most of the qualifying criteria you look for, yet has a fairly extended period of time left before their current contract expires. You should begin the sales cycle with a "Thank You" letter, and enter them into your "Tickler" file for follow-up with a letter/call every 60 to 75 days (depending on their contract expiration). Save your best tools for the last 90 days.

"HAPPY WITHOUT YOU"

This prospect is similar to the "Currently Committed." They may be happy with the incumbent vendor, or a nonuser who is not aware of the potential benefit of using your product or service. If you know that they use a lot of your product/service, you want to lavish them with attention, just like the "Currently Committed," except on a different schedule. You might want to spread out your calls and letters over a longer period, like every four months.

"HARD TO GET"

Since you can't make contact, you don't really know enough to determine whether you would jump off of a cliff for this prospect, but if you know that they are in the right line of business and probably would benefit from your service. You might have to call at different times of the day before relying on the mail (don't leave messages every time, just occasionally so that they recognize your name, or you may annoy your intended).

In some cases, the person you contact may simply be having a bad day. For instance, if the person you talk to is unreceptive, but not downright rude, they should be filed for a call in about a month-and-a-half. You should also send them a letter about a week before you call. Hopefully, you will catch them in a better mood at some point.

Figure 2.3.1

"HARD TO FORGET"

You know that this company uses enormous amounts of your product or service, so you want to put a little more work into them, as demonstrated in the Truebeep case study. You want to send them some information, but you should also do some homework to see if perhaps there are other departments/branches/divisions that you could penetrate (refer to Figure 2.3.2). If you can get your foot in the door, even if it is just a small order, you will have a much better chance of eventually penetrating the organization. An internal reference will give you a substantial edge over other salespeople when the time comes to bid on the more significant business within the same company.

"HAPPY WITHOUT THEM"

Don't waste a lot of time on a prospect that is deliriously happy with their current vendor/alternative, and/or is under a long-term contract, and especially if they are paying significantly less than you would need to ask for your product/service. If you have no edge at all, keep the lead in a competitor file.

You can reactivate the lead if you find out that the competitor has dropped the ball badly with other customers, like if their billing system becomes a nightmare, or their customer service department is having major problems fulfilling their customers' needs. Naturally, the same holds true if you find out that the account manager that they were loyal to has left the company.

Figure 2.3.1 (Continued)

When you attempt to penetrate a prospective company, always start by trying to contact someone in as high a position as you can in the organization, and then work backwards if necessary. While the specific titles within organizations may be somewhat different, most organizations will have the types of key management and staff positions listed in Figure 2.3.2.

A Traditional Organization Structure

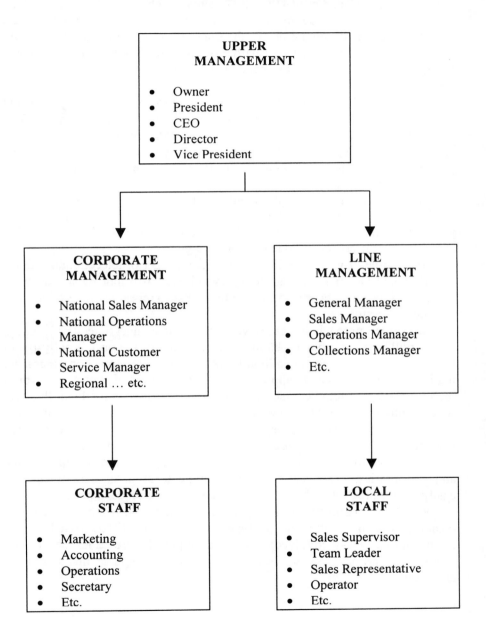

Figure 2.3.2

Some people are of the opinion that it is impossible to get through to upper level management, and/or that they are swamped with sales solicitations. While a CEO usually does have an executive secretary to screen out time-wasters, that can be a plus if you are one of the salespeople who does get through. As far as being swamped, that is usually not the case. Since many salespeople think that they are probably swamped, they usually contact someone at a lower level.

Even if the CEO or vice president refers you to someone else, you would have their endorsement, and since your original contact is probably the final decision-maker, the person they refer you to will probably take you more seriously. We will discuss the issue of who you contact and how their particular role in the organization will affect your strategy in much greater detail in the next chapter.

There are usually multiple management roles at each level of the organization, such as a VP of Sales, VP of Operations, etc., so when you can't get through to one contact at that level, you should consider approaching someone in a different department before you give up.

For example, if you normally go after the manager of telecommunications, but are unable to make contact after several tries, why not move on to the manager of the next department, like MIS, and keep repeating the process until you are successful.

Using this approach increases your potential contact rate dramatically, which will increase your probability of penetration. If you normally try to make contact six times per individual before you give up (phone message, mail, fax, and/or email), approaching four different departments would increase your attempted contact level to 24 times. There is no doubt that you will eventually penetrate somewhere in the organization with that many tries. Again, this level of prospecting activity is only recommended when you are pretty sure that you are pursuing a viable major prospect.

In addition, major companies often have multiple locations, departments, and subsidiaries. What starts out as a single location or department can easily be nurtured into a fast-growing, multiple location customer.

Every large organization has a person or department responsible for key business functions, although the type of department differs based on the organizational tasks involved. As an example, Figure 2.3.3 shows the various departments you could target in a typical manufacturing environment.

Departmental Structure

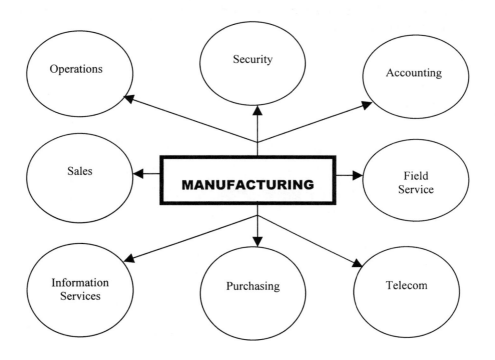

Figure 2.3.3

Needless to say, if you have to deliver some new business immediately, you should temporarily delay working on your large prospects until you close some smaller accounts with shorter buying cycles. Once you have a lot of large, qualified prospects in the hopper, you can stop working on the very small accounts without experiencing long dry spells. We discuss performance planning in much greater detail in Chapter Four.

I also want to make a couple of suggestions about dealing with competitors. As I mentioned in "Happy Without You" (Figure 2.3.1), when you can't take a customer away from a competitor after trying everything you can think of, keep the lead in case something changes in the future, like the quality of a competitor's customer service deteriorating. If you use index cards, highlight the top edge of the cards with a different color for each competitor so that you can easily find them if something changes.

Also, make sure that you keep abreast of your competitor's strengths and weaknesses so you know how to beat a particular competitor when you run into him and, just as important, so you will also know when you can't possibly win a particular account.

Let's take a look at some examples of different types of letters you can fax or mail to your prospects.

*   *   *

TOPIC 2.3: Case Study

Scenario #1

Prospect: Association of the Romantically Deprived

You stop by the association headquarters while you are in the area for another meeting and find out that Frank Lonelee, the telecommunications manager, is responsible for the association's paging services. You are unable to get through to him directly after leaving a message about once a week for three weeks.

Of course, you also called at different times, but without leaving a message, so that they wouldn't know how anxious you are. It's a good thing you made a note of the date and time of each call.

After three weeks, you mail the introduction letter that follows, with a brochure. (We'll skip the brochure).

TRUEBEEP CORPORATION
The paging solutions company

June 8, 1999

Mr. Frank Lee Lonelee
Association of the Romantically Deprived
6200 Love Drive
Romance, Maryland 20000

Dear Frank;

As an Association Paging Services Specialist for Truebeep Corporation, I am very interested in finding out whether our service would be as beneficial for your association as it is for our other clients. I know that you are very busy, so I have enclosed some information for your review.

As the nation's leading paging company, Truebeep has the resources to provide unparalleled service, and the latest technology, including international wireless satellite communications, and interactive two-way paging. Personally, I am excited by Truebeep's customer service commitment. We have a Major Accounts Program that is designed to provide specialized billing and support, and we can create a custom wireless network for your specialized needs.

I look forward to meeting with you so that I might better understand your communications requirements. Should circumstances cause your paging system to become a high priority before I am able to connect with you, please call me at (301) 555-9999.

Sincerely,

Alan Salesperson
Association Paging Services Specialist

Enclosure
AS/twp

100 Beep Boulevard . Pageheaven . Maryland . 20003 . (301) 999-6666

Instead of writing a new letter for each situation that you uncover, some very simple changes to the same basic letter can make it appropriate for most of the common situations you encounter. Some examples follow, and I have made the changes in the respective letters bold so that you can see how the minor changes totally refocus the message.

First, let's look at a letter that you can use for the most common response that we all get while prospecting. When someone tells you to send some information, they may be trying to get rid of you, but some are very serious and always conduct business that way. In fact, I typically ask salespeople for information before I meet with them so that I can prepare a set of questions.

Since it takes only a moment to change the name and address on a basic letter that you reuse, it is no big deal to respond so that you can get an appointment with those prospects who are serious. Even if they file your letter in the "circular file," their guilt about throwing away your letter may give you a little leverage into the account.

Make sure that you send them some information while they still remember asking for it, and follow up with a call in about five days.

[Information Request]

TRUEBEEPCORPORATION
The paging solutions company

June 8, 1999

Mr. Frank Lee Lonelee
Association of the Romantically Deprived
6200 Love Drive
Romance, Maryland 20000

Dear Frank;

As per your request, I have enclosed some information for your review. As an Association Paging Services Specialist for Truebeep Corporation, I am very interested in finding out whether our service would be as beneficial for your association as it is for our other clients.

As the nation's leading paging company, Truebeep has the resources to provide unparalleled service, and the latest technology, including international wireless satellite communications, and interactive two-way paging. Personally, I am excited by Truebeep's customer service commitment. We have a Major Accounts Program that is designed to provide specialized billing and support, and we can create a custom wireless network for your specialized needs.

I look forward to meeting with you so that I might better understand your communications requirements. Should circumstances cause your paging system to become a high priority before I am able to connect with you, please call me at (301) 555-9999.

Sincerely,

Alan Salesperson
Association Paging Services Specialist

Enclosure
AS/twp

[Non-User]

TRUEBEEPCORPORATION
The paging solutions company

June 8, 1999

Mr. Frank Lee Lonelee
Association of the Romantically Deprived
6200 Love Drive
Romance, Maryland 20000

Dear Frank;

As an Association Paging Services Specialist for Truebeep Corporation, I am very interested in finding out whether our service would be as beneficial for your association as it is for our other clients. I know that you are very busy, so I have therefore enclosed some information for your review.

As the nation's leading paging company, Truebeep has the resources to provide unparalleled service, and the latest technology, including international wireless satellite communications, and interactive two-way paging. Personally, I am excited by Truebeep's customer service commitment. We have a Major Accounts Program that is designed to provide specialized billing and support, and we can create a custom wireless network for your specialized needs.

Although I understand that you do not use pagers, I would appreciate it if you could spare a few minutes so that I can show you what we have done for other companies in your industry. I look forward to meeting with you so that I might better understand your communications requirements. If you have any questions, please call me at (301) 555-9999.

Sincerely,

Alan Salesperson
Association Paging Services Specialist

Enclosure
AS/twp

100 Beep Boulevard . Pageheaven . Maryland . 20003 . (301) 999-6666

[Referral]

TRUEBEEP CORPORATION
The paging solutions company

June 8, 1997

Ms. Candy Cane
PiggOut Foods, Inc.
8000 Gourmet Plaza
Abundance, Maryland 30000

Dear Candy;

In a recent conversation with Frank Lonelee at the Association of the Romantically Deprived, he suggested that you might have a need for our paging services, so I wanted to get some information to you. I am very interested in finding out whether our service would be as beneficial for your organization as it has been for our other clients.

As the nation's leading paging company, Truebeep has the resources to provide unparalleled service, and the latest technology, including international wireless satellite communications, and interactive two-way paging. Personally, I am excited by Truebeep's customer service commitment. We have a Major Accounts Program that is designed to provide specialized billing and support, and we can create a custom wireless network for your specialized needs.

I look forward to meeting with you so that I might better understand your communications requirements. Should circumstances cause your paging system to become a high priority before I am able to connect with you, please call me at (301) 555-9999.

Sincerely,

Alan Salesperson
Paging Services Specialist

Enclosure
AS/twp

Scenario #2

Prospect: NetCom

You make a phone call to NetCom and learn that John Hogg is the Vice President of Telecommunications. As usual, you are unable to get through to him directly.

You decide to send him a letter, but you make a very small change. Since you work with a lot of associations, your company has designated you as the "association specialist," but you decide that it isn't necessary to include that title in your letter to John. That is really the only thing that you chance in your basic letter (why keep reinventing the wheel?).

NOTE: To avoid unnecessary suffering, I won't keep duplicating the other examples of correspondence for both the association and NetCom, just the key sections like the strategy.

TRUEBEEP CORPORATION
The paging solutions company

June 8, 1999

Mr. John Hogg
NetCom Corporation
1616 Hi-Tech Boulevard
Baltimore, Maryland 20000

Dear John;

As a Paging Services Specialist for Truebeep Corporation, I am very interested in finding out whether our service would be as beneficial for your organization as it is for our other clients. I know that you are very busy, so I have enclosed some information for your review.

As the nation's leading paging company, Truebeep has the resources to provide unparalleled service, and the latest technology, including international wireless satellite communications, and interactive two-way paging. Personally, I am excited by Truebeep's customer service commitment. We have a Major Accounts Program that is designed to provide specialized billing and support, and we can create a custom wireless network for your specialized needs.

I look forward to meeting with you so that I might better understand your communications requirements. Should circumstances cause your paging system to become a high priority before I am able to connect with you, please call me at (301) 555-9999.

Sincerely,

Alan Salesperson
Paging Services Specialist

Enclosure
AS/twp

TOPIC 2.3: Exercise

1. List the buying centers for one of your vertical markets:

_____

_____

_____

_____

_____

_____

2. When do you normally schedule your prospecting activities?

_____

_____

3. What do you do when other activities interfere?

_____

_____

4. When do you sort and organize leads?

_____

_____

Answer Key: Page 268
Disk: Exercise Folder

TOPIC 2.3: Assignment

❏ Find out whether the large customers you are currently working with have any other departments or divisions that you can target where you can use your contact as a reference. Add that information to Column 3 of your major customer list on Page 26.

❏ Do the same thing with the top 20 suspects on your target list, and add the information to the last column on Page 27.

❏ Classify the prospects you are working on, and develop a contact schedule and strategy, taking into account whether there are any conditions you are aware of (like contractual obligations, etc.) that would indicate a firm decision date and/or influence the timing of your steps.

Disk: Assignment Folder

CHAPTER 2: High-Impact Prospecting

TOPIC 2.4: Vertical Market Penetration

SKILLSET TOPIC(S)
☐ Understanding vertical market dynamics
☐ Developing industry-specific strategies
☐ Writing a business plan to justify capital investments

OBJECTIVE

To teach you how to eliminate any specific vertical market obstacles that might impair your ability to sell to organizations within that industry, and/or leverage any advantages that you may uncover.

BENEFITS

✓ Eliminate industry-specific obstacles.
✓ Better understand vertical market dynamics.
✓ Develop effective industry penetration strategies.
✓ Increase approval of capital investments.
✓ Become an industry specialist.

> *"If any aspect of your product or service is unique, you can eliminate competitors by getting your contact to specify in the bid that your unique feature is mandatory for any party to participate."*

Occasionally, there are special circumstances that affect your ability to get an appointment when you are targeting a specific industry, in which case you might have to develop a specific penetration strategy.

Once you have gone on a few appointments with prospects in a particular industry, you will be able to find out if there are any special conditions that you need to resolve, or needs that you can use to effectively compete for their business.

Example 2.4.1 looks at the government market, a high-priority target for most vendors.

Selling to the government is a little different than selling to most companies in the private sector, although certain aspects are still the same. For example, they will still be more likely to do business with you if you appear to be a knowledgeable professional, and it always helps if they like you.

In order to break into the government market, you need to develop a list of the agencies that have an office in your territory, even though purchasing may originate from another location (which is usually in Philadelphia).

You will sometimes have to pass through a security gate, so you need to make an appointment with someone by phone instead of cold-calling.

Even though most government bids are decided by bid, you will face less competition when your company has been approved as a preferred vendor or is listed on a GSA schedule. If not, you may want to help them become approved. Once you establish an account you will seldom face competition at renewal time if you have done a good job of supporting the account. That is one of the reasons why so many companies try to sell to the government.

As in any situation, if your contact is required to submit at least three bids, you might want to suggest that they review bids from competitors that you know are either more expensive, or unable to meet the specifications. I call that tactic "Bracketing" the bid. This strategy will not work unless your contact really likes and respects you as a professional.

You can also eliminate competitors if there is any aspect of your product/ service/ support that is unique. All you have to do is get your contact to specify in the bid that your unique feature is mandatory for any party to be eligible to participate in the bidding process.

As an example, if your company exclusively offered pink beepers that whistled *Dixie*, you would want to try to get the bid written in such a language that every vendor who bid had to offer pink beepers that whistled. (Which is probably how hammers ended up costing the government $500.00 each, and they don't even whistle.)

Doing this type of preparatory work will greatly improve your ability to be effective in a specific vertical market, and may even be critical when pursuing some markets. Assuming, again, that you sell paging services, you might develop the penetration strategy that follows if certain conditions existed based on what you discover about government buying patterns, and related issues that affect your ability to sell them paging.

Target #1: THE FEDERAL GOVERNMENT

CONDITIONS
- Federal government purchasing agency decision-makers are normally required to put contracts valued at over $10,000.00 to bid annually, and are mandated to accept the lowest bid (unless a higher bid is justified by some exclusive aspect of the vendor's product or service).

STRATEGY
- Get referrals from established government accounts.
- Talk to other salespeople who handle government accounts to find out what they are doing.
- Identify other user agencies (request a list from a GSA contact).
- Get on various agencies' bidders' lists.
- Pursue GSA scheduling qualifications.

TARGET QUALIFIERS
- Transactions under $10,000 (annual P.O./purchase total).
- Referrals from current government accounts.
- Agencies that primarily use local or wide-area services (metro area).

TECHNIQUE
- Begin sales cycle 75 to 90 days before contract renewal date.
- Establish credibility/value of your company's Federal System Program.
- Help your contact specify certain criteria in the bid specifications that would disqualify your competitors from being able to bid, because they would be unable to provide that service. (Do a competitive survey to establish what your competitor's weaknesses are).
- Research your competitors to identify those that you can beat in areas such as price, product/service capabilities, and support, so that you know when you have an advantage.

Example 2.4.1

Example 2.4.2 addresses the medical market, which ranks second in the private sector on the paging target list, and is also a great example of an industry with unusual conditions. As a result of the life-and-death nature of the profession, hospitals need certain key features in their communications equipment/service, and some are mandatory for any communications company to qualify to participate in the bidding process.

You would have to develop a different strategy than the one for military targets, as in the example that follows.

Target #2: THE MEDICAL MARKET

CONDITIONS
➤ Hospitals often have both in-house and remote paging systems.
➤ Emergency response personnel need high priority.
➤ 24-hour system engineering support is required.
➤ Immediate turnaround on defective beeper replacement is expected.
➤ Penetration in hospital basements is often a problem due to radiation shielding.

STRATEGY
You decide to get your company to offer a special package to the hospitals in your market, with special features that take into account the specific needs of the profession (we'll talk about how to get your company to spend their money next). Don't worry too much about the technical jargon, just think of the special things that you have had to do for some of your clients in the past. Your medical package might look like this:
➤ In-house transmitter/antenna (where justified by number of pagers).
➤ Remote programming terminal for 24-hour service.
➤ Redundancy for system backup, with automatic transfer in the event of failure.
➤ Fail-safe power source for terminal and link transmitter.
➤ Alarms tied to terminals and transmitters for system failure notification.
➤ Dedicated telephone lines to hospital, with automatic rerouting to external trunks in event of problems.
➤ Hot and cold spare pagers on-site.
➤ Group rate for hospital employee enrollment.

TARGET QUALIFIERS
➤ Transactions over $50,000 (to cover special expenses).
➤ Referrals from current hospital accounts.
➤ Hospitals that primarily use local or wide-area services (metro area).

TECHNIQUE
➤ Begin sales cycle 75 to 90 days before contract renewal date.
➤ Establish credibility/value of your Major Account/Hospital Program (even if you are the only major account/hospital representative in your company).

> ➤ Help develop criteria for bid specifications that might disqualify your competitors from being able to bid because they would be unable to provide that service.
> ➤ Research your competitors to determine who has weaknesses that you can take advantage of.
> ➤ Talk to other offices for hospital references in strong markets.
> ➤ Presentation/proposal tailored for medical market.
> ➤ Find out about other applications used in hospital accounts from co-workers, and from salespeople in other cities.

Example 2.4.2

Finally, let's look at a tool that you might want to use if your company has to lay out some capital in order to provide a specific product or feature that a key vertical market may require, as in the preceding medical market example.

If at first your manager says that they can't justify the expense, there is a way to get them to make the investment. Many managers will go to bat for you if you give them ammunition in the form of potential revenue or a market analysis. An example of each follows:

POTENTIAL REVENUE PROJECTION

SITUATION: You are trying to sell pagers to a hospital, but you don't beep in part of the building.

SOLUTION: You need to install a transmitter on or near the building.

PROBLEM: It would cost $30,000.00

STRATEGY: When you approach your supervisor, you have to do more than just explain the need. To open their checkbook, you will get the best results if you can demonstrate the benefit to your company and/or the potential return on investment it will realize by penetrating that account.

EXAMPLE: The hospital would order 1,000 pagers (mixed types), with an average monthly rate of $10.00, or $10,000.00 per month. Since the hospital would agree to a three-year contract, the value of the agreement would be $360,000.00. In addition, the hospital is affiliated with several others, so there would be potential for additional business (use the same formula to calculate value).

NEW TARGET MARKET ANALYSIS

Exhibit A

MEDICAL MARKET SURVEY

A recent survey of 181 companies contacted in the medical field (including customers) yielded the following information:

SIZE	TOTAL #		RENTALS		OWNED	
Range	#Accts	#Pagers	#Accts	#Pagers	#Accts	#Pagers
15-50	112	4,040	79	2,700	43	1,300
%*	66%	41%				
51-100	38	2,845	26	1,965	12	880
%	20%	29%				
100+	19	2,850	11	1,650	8	1,200
%	10%	24%				
TOTALS	181	9,735	116	6,355	65	3,380
%			64%		36%	

Once you have the basic statistics you can do an analysis of those facts, as represented on the next page. Your objective is to make it really easy for your boss to present the information to his or her boss. As long as your statistics are presented in a clear manner, the accountants can crunch the numbers to determine the potential return on the proposed investment.

This is also a great tool to get special pricing for one of your prospects. If a company or organization has multiple locations, you can use the same format to show your boss how much future business the company might win if it approves special group rates. We will discuss this strategy later.

NEW TARGET MARKET ANALYSIS

Exhibit B

MEDICAL MARKETING RECOMMENDATIONS

SUMMARY:
- 48% of accounts sampled fit into 30- to 75-unit category
- Represents 42% of units accounted for in survey
- 30% of total units are rental, and conform to the 30- to 75-unit account size range

EVALUATION:
- The 30- to 75-unit accounts represent the best opportunities, and there are 3,380 units available in approximately 10% of the vertical market, which extrapolates into a total potential of 33,000 units

RECOMMENDATION:
- By investing in --------, which we need to win their business, we have a chance to win at least ----- worth of business, even if we only win X% of the available business, etc.

NOTE: These percentages relate to a sample group developed from our customer base, prospects that we are pursuing, and those lost for the reasons listed above.

Using hard numbers should excite your boss. While not mandatory, it will impress your manager more if you use a presentation that includes charts and/or graphs. The supporting statistics that you use might be less complicated, and can come from any sources that seem appropriate. Be creative, but use verifiable sources where possible.

*   *   *

TOPIC 2.4: Assignment

❑ Select two key industries that you would like focus on from the group that you have already listed (select industries where you have a working knowledge of their specific issues).

❑ Based on your experience with other companies in those industries, develop a vertical market strategy for each that takes into account the various special circumstances that you might have to deal with.

Target #1: _____

CONDITIONS

STRATEGY

TARGET QUALIFIERS

TECHNIQUE

Target #2: _____

<u>**CONDITIONS**</u>

<u>**STRATEGY**</u>

<u>**TARGET QUALIFIERS**</u>

<u>**TECHNIQUE**</u>

Disk: Assignment Folder

CHAPTER 2: High-Impact Prospecting

TOPIC 2.5: Lead Management

SKILLSET TOPIC(S)
- ❑ Designing an effective lead management system
- ❑ Assigning activity codes
- ❑ Making the system user-friendly

OBJECTIVE

To provide you with the tools to enable you to keep track of the prospects you are working on, as well as those you might be able to develop a relationship with in the future as their situation changes and your skill level improves.

BENEFITS

- ✓ Track and respond to prospects' needs in a timely fashion.
- ✓ Simplify and improve your record-keeping.
- ✓ Prevent leads from becoming lost between the cracks.
- ✓ Avoid staleness cold streaks.
- ✓ Become better at displacing your competitors.

> "If you manage your leads effectively you will have information about virtually every major prospect in your territory, even those that you lose."

In many ways, the database that you use to keep track of sales leads is like your "little black book." Other than being a lot larger, the only real difference is that you don't throw your database away when you get married.

Since there are relatively few major accounts out there, you can't afford to lose track of any of them, so your database really is indispensable.

Keeping track of the leads you develop is especially critical when you start a new job, because you will usually have plenty of time to prospect at first, and no spare time at all once you have a lot of accounts to manage.

If you manage your leads effectively, once you are established you will have information about virtually every major prospect in the territory, including those that you lose. When you go back to rebid them a year later, you will be better prepared and have a much better chance of winning the account.

Another benefit that many salespeople can really appreciate is that once you develop an effective lead management system, it will progressively reduce the cold prospecting that you have to do.

If you already have a computer, or you have access to one at work, the easiest way to set up a lead contact system is to buy a contact management software program. The program I use is ACT. It will automatically notify me when some follow-up action is required or scheduled for a given lead. I can store tons of information in the Comments section, and pull up specific leads or special groups by entering key criteria for a search. The ACT program also lets me generate mailing lists and print form letters, envelopes, and labels.

There are some great packages out there, and the features I have just described in ACT are fairly standard, so I am not going to go into great detail about them. If you decide to get one of the contact management programs, I recommend that you do some shopping. I have included some information on a few of the available programs in the Appendix, and you can find out more about them at any computer store.

If you are considering getting a computer, using it for lead tracking alone will more than pay for the investment, and it will be extremely handy to develop some of the other sales tools that we will cover later.

The other alternative is to use an index card system, which I will elaborate on since you will have to design this type of system yourself. Even if you automate your database, it is a good idea to keep a hard copy for backup. Index cards are also really convenient when you are in the field, for recording critical information until you have a chance to update your computer records. Figure 2.5.1 illustrates how you might organize your lead system.

Database Design

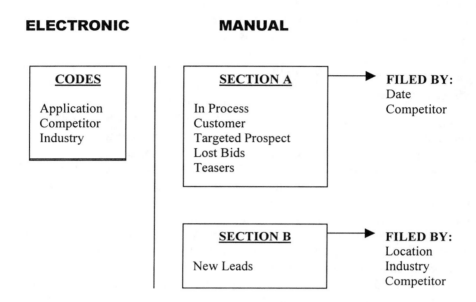

Figure 2.5.1

If you use a manual system, you can get index cards, dividers, and lead boxes of various sizes at any stationery supply store. Based on the amount of information required, 3 x 5 cards are the most common, although you can use larger cards if you need to have a lot of information available while you are in the field.

You need to organize your lead cards so that your system is easy to use. Your primary section should be organized according to the follow-up date of any scheduled activities for each prospect, with monthly and daily tabs. You can then file leads by the date in the month that you need to follow up. At the end of each month, you simply take the next month's scheduled action leads and file them in the appropriate day of the coming month.

My personal hard copy backup system has three sections, including the follow-up section just described. I also file targeted accounts I have not yet contacted by zip code so that I can call them when I am planning to be nearby. Finally, my customers are filed alphabetically in a different section. You may want to file your targeted accounts by vertical market, or use some other criteria that better suit your needs. As I mentioned earlier, I also color the top edge of each card with a different color for each competitor.

You have to record the same information on index cards that you would use in an electronic contact management system, information that will enable you to review scheduled contacts for each upcoming day. That way you can plan what to say based upon what your objective is for calling: whether it is a follow-up to some previous action, or an initial penetration.

You can also plan your day around the leads filed for future contact by calling other prospects that are in the same general geographic area as your scheduled appointments. Even better, if you call other companies in the same industry, you will pick up on industry norms and eccentricities that might exist. You can then use their language, and you will appear to be an expert.

Your index card might look like this:

Sample Lead Card

[FRONT]

```
Assn. of the Romantically Deprived
6200 Love Drive
Romance, MD 20000
555-9999
CONTACT: Frank Lonelee


ML#1   3/11/99
LM     3/18/99
TC     3/21/99
```

[REAR]

```
Don't know how many pagers, but another
association account that we have has over
1,500 pagers, which would be... boy, am I
feeling romantic. That's three months quota.
```

Whether you use a lead management program or an index card system, make sure you record what actions you have taken, any letters you have sent, what happened with the lead, and what you need to do next.

Since lead cards have limited space, you may want to code repetitive activities. I have included some examples of codes you can use to keep track of your activity in Table 2.5.1.

CONTACT CODES

❏ TC - Telephone contact
❏ LM - Left message
❏ TS - Telephone survey
❏ SS - Site survey (blind date)
❏ CC - Cold call
❏ PR - Proposal generated
❏ SP - Sales presentation
❏ ML - Mailed letter
❏ MX - Mailed Christmas card
❏ NA - No answer (write down the time so you can call at different times)
❏ NI - Not interested
❏ CB - Call back (write down date/time)

Table 2.5.1

Using codes will enable you to do several things. You will be able to record a lot of history with minimum effort, and avoid duplicating activities with the same client when they take a long time to close. For instance, your code for a particular letter that you send might be ML#3 1/1/99, indicating that you mailed letter #3 on 1/1/99. That way, when you look at your notes, you would know at a glance which letter you sent, what has happened, and what you had planned for your next scheduled call. Using this type of system enables you to easily make the transition to the next step, regardless of how long it takes between steps (which is especially useful if the sale takes from six months to a year to close).

You should also take notes during your meetings and conversations. For example, if a prospect tells you that he/she will be out of town because their daughter is going into the hospital, when next you talk to them you can inquire as to the result of the operation. I even make personal notes about my contact, like if they are a sailboat enthusiast, so that I can pick out a Thank You card with a sailboat on it, or clip articles about sailing, golf, etc.

If you really want to maximize your productivity, make sure that you keep your prime hours free to call prospects and customers. While you want to update your database consistently, try to do it during the evenings and early morning instead of during those periods when you could be talking to customers and prospects.

The leads you have filed for future action could be considered "warm," since you probably have a contact name, if not additional information about their circumstances that you could use in conversation. Mixing some of them in with your "cold calls" will break up the monotony and neutralize the occasional "cold shoulder" shock that we all experience.

Although it can be a lot of work, your database will prove to be invaluable. I once calculated that I made around 30 dollars an hour for every hour I spent working on my database, which is not a bad part-time salary since most of it was done in the evenings or early in the morning, which did not interfere with other activities.

*   *   *

TOPIC 2.5: Assignment

1. List any industries where your company has an edge against your largest competitors.

2. Rate your product/service/company's competitive strengths and weaknesses against the competitors you face most often.

Competitor	Your strengths	Your weaknesses
#1		
#2		
#3		

Disk: Assignment Folder

CHAPTER THREE

The Anatomy of an Effective Strategy

"Salespeople must have a masochistic streak, because one minute they will be talking about the painful, frustrating pursuit of some major account, and the next minute they are out the door like a shot when one of their large prospects says that they are ready to take bids."

CHAPTER 3: Anatomy of an Effective Strategy

TOPIC 3.1: Qualifying the Prospect

SKILLSET TOPIC(s)
- ❑ Establishing effective qualifying criteria
- ❑ Review of the opening presentation
- ❑ Scripting a fact-finding survey
- ❑ Prospect data analysis

OBJECTIVE
To help you develop a system to qualify a prospect, eliminate time-wasters, gather sufficient information to prioritize effectively, and develop a winning strategy and action plan.

BENEFITS
- ✓ Establish effective qualifying criteria.
- ✓ Create a powerful opening presentation.
- ✓ Eliminate time wasted on unqualified prospects.
- ✓ Get more effective information for your strategy and the resulting action plan.
- ✓ Improve project prioritization.

> *"If you fail to qualify your prospect at the beginning of the relationship, you could end up wasting valuable time, which does not help your performance or your bank account."*

As you know, the first meeting with any prospective client can be somewhat unpredictable. In fact, when the account is really large, the only things you can count on are butterflies and the probability that you will have a bad hair day. Is that any different than a hot date?

Unless you prepare a list of questions before you go on the initial appointment, that unpredictability makes it easy to miss key information. Without adequate information, you have to rely on instinct, which is okay for dating, but not when it comes to qualifying a prospect. Actually, in my personal experience, gut instincts do not always work that well in romance either.

Needless to say, if you fail to qualify your prospect at the beginning of the relationship, you could end up wasting valuable time, which would directly affect your performance, and not help your bank account a bit.

When I first started in sales, I used to get excited when I found a suspect that would talk to me. And if they were unhappy with their current vendor, I figured that it was a done deal. Needless to say, I missed a lot of sales forecasts. It took quite a while before I learned how to distinguish between qualified prospects and unqualified suspects. I still get excited when someone is willing to talk to me, but I don't forecast it as a sale until I get a lot more information. And that means I have to get them talking.

The introduction that follows has helped me get a prospect to become a chatterbox, and you should be able to get the same results by using it. When you go on the first sales call with a new prospect, you want to disclose your purpose in a clear, concise way. That would include why you're there, what you want to accomplish, and what you're capable (and not capable) of doing. You also need to explain how you intend to proceed, and how you both might expect to benefit from the relationship.

That represents a self-disclosure statement, which will help establish your credibility so that your prospect will believe that you are competent to solve any problem that you might uncover.

For example, you might start your first meeting with Frank Lonelee at the Association of the Romantically Deprived with the presentation that follows.

Setting the Mood

STATEMENT OF PURPOSE:

"Mr. Lonelee, at Truebeep we believe that the purpose of a business is to solve problems, and the reason for my visit today is to see if we might be able to help you and your organization increase the efficiency of your paging network, and possibly decrease your cost."

ESTABLISHING CREDIBILITY:

"In preparing for this meeting, I tried to put myself in your position. Since we've never met before, and you're not currently doing business with Truebeep, I thought you might be wondering a little about who I am, what our company does, how we do business and, most of all, what Truebeep can do for your company that someone else can't do better.

"Well, we are in the business of solving communications problems for people who need to be contacted when they are away from the office. Our approach has traditionally been different from others in the industry in that we prefer to take a consultative approach, identifying a problem to be solved. We're not interested in selling you unless it creates a win-win situation for all parties.

"I personally am part of a marketing team that has over 100 years of experience, experience that has positioned Truebeep as one of the strongest-growing communications companies in the country. And not by accident. We're innovative in terms of offering systems and services that are reliable, and we back that up with what we think is exceptional dedication and commitment to customer support."

(Describe your knowledge of the customer's organization and his/her business, and build rapport by asking about their position, which also helps you rate your potential conquest.)

DESCRIBING YOUR METHOD:

"Would it be alright if I just take a moment and tell you how we like to conduct business?

"First, I'd like to ask you some questions to find out about everything that is important to you, and to see if there is a 'fit' between our organizations. If there is, then I'll suggest some solutions in the form of options and alternatives for you to consider. The final decision will, of course, be yours."

EXPLAINING THE BENEFIT:

"If there isn't a match between our two companies, then you'll know that you are already operating as efficiently as possible. If you decide on one of the options that we'll discuss, I'll do everything necessary to insure a smooth implementation. Your paging service will be enhanced, and you'll operate even more efficiently. I'll have a new customer, ongoing revenue, and a source for referrals.

"Now, if that sounds reasonable to you, could I ask you some questions? Also, because the time we spend together and what you say is important to me, may I take some notes as we talk?"

You can easily plug your own facts into the preceding presentation. Once you have earned the right to continue, you are ready for the next phase. In a way, this is the most critical part of the sales cycle, because the information that you get will determine your ultimate success in selling your product/service to that prospect.

When you leave the first meeting you need to know whether the prospect is qualified, and if they are, you need to know how the company uses your product/service, as well as what problem(s) or application(s) exist that you can solve, or at least improve. That information will basically set the platform for the sale.

While some prospects will automatically provide you with everything that you need to know, and a few will tell you a lot more than you ever wanted to know, with most prospects you have to ask the right questions. In addition to getting good information, that will also demonstrate a high level of professionalism to your contact.

First, let's make sure you spend your time with the right prospects by doing a brief review of the qualifying fundamentals. I'm sure you would agree that for a prospect to be qualified they have to have a problem that you can solve, or an application where your product/service can benefit the company. They may not know it yet, but they will by the time you propose.

In situations where no problem exists, and there is no special application for your product/service, there really is no reason for a company to make a change at that time. Don't devote too much energy to those prospects, but file them away in case something changes, as we discussed earlier.

Some of the criteria that would eliminate a prospect would include:

NOT

✓ The company does not have a need that you can satisfy better than their current vendor or the alternative that they are using.

✓ They have a vendor/account manager that they are pleased with, and they are paying less than you could possibly get approved (unless their wants are such that you could justify the increased cost). These prospects should be filed for a six-month follow-up contact. If you are using index cards, you should color-code them along with other loyal customers of that particular competitor. That way you can find them instantly if that competitor stumbles.

✓ They have a year or more left on their contract, in which case you would put them on a 90-day contact schedule.

✓ They are going bankrupt, or have severe financial difficulties. Don't try too hard to get credit approval because if they don't pay, you won't get paid. The time you invest to sell, deliver, and manage the account will be wasted.

That sums up the situations that you want to avoid, with one exception. When a prospect needs some product or service that you don't offer, before you write them off you should try to get your company to add that product, service, or feature by using a market analysis and revenue projection (as demonstrated in the Medical Market example).

Except for that particular type of situation, when the prospect is unqualified you should recommend that they stay with their current vendor, or find another vendor who would be a better match. While it might be tempting to try to sell them anyway in the hopes that it will work out, that approach will usually end up bringing you a lot of grief. Winning an account when you know that you will not be able to provide adequate solutions to their problems just puts everyone in a losing situation.

Another benefit of being honest and walking away from the sale is that the prospective buyer will respect you and will be more likely to give you referrals. Although many salespeople fail to ask for referrals in that situation because they just assume that an unqualified prospect wouldn't give them any, that is not always the case. If the prospect you are talking to is unqualified because of some feature that you don't offer, or because they would not benefit from the use of your product/service, they probably know someone else with different circumstances that would make them a viable prospect.

Now let's talk about qualified prospects. The list that follows covers most of the positive variables that you might run into, any one of which would indicate that you have uncovered a viable situation:

HIGH PROBABILITY PROSPECTS

✓ They have a recognized or unidentified need for your product or service.

✓ They have a budget for, and/or the ability to pay for, your product or service.

✓ Your contact has the ability to make or influence the purchase decision.

✓ You make a good emotional connection with your contact.

✓ They have an incumbent vendor/competitor that you are superior to because of leverage strengths, things like your product/service being more efficient, and/or proven superior in productivity improvement, etc. Having better pricing than the current vendor is always a plus, although you still have do a good job because it is sometimes amazing how creative the incumbent sales managers can become at the threat of losing a really large or high-profile account.

✓ Your product/service provides a unique feature or capability that the client needs. I think that is always the best position to be in, because if the organization needs a specific solution that nobody else can provide, you will typically have a lot more flexibility with pricing.

✓ They are reviewing their current vendor agreement (don't you love it when you get lucky?).

✓ Their contract will be expiring soon (and you will have some sort of an edge).

✓ There is a weakness in your competitor's position, like poor customer support, billing problems, shipping delays, long hold-time for callers.

✓ They don't have an account manager, or don't know who it is. (Don't forget to ask, because they might be used to poor service and not associate it with anyone; but they will know if they have become an orphan account where the salesperson has moved on and they no longer see a live person).

✓ If they actually don't like their account manager, I usually check to see if I am dreaming.

✓ You have satisfied customers with exactly the same application/ in the same industry who currently benefit from a specialized application of your company's service (and who will be enthusiastic if contacted by your prospect).

✓ In the perfect situation, you will be the only vendor who can offer your prospect this specialized application.

As you know, any prospective buyer is qualified if he can benefit from using your product/service and pay for it, but the fact is, some prospects are more qualified than others. For instance, if a suspect has any one of the above circumstances, like the fact that they are getting bids, they are qualified. However, if a combination of two positive variables exists, such as they are getting bids and are having problems with billing, your odds of making the sale become a little bit better because they are more likely to make a change.

When a prospect has more than two positive indicators, like they are shopping for a new vendor, they currently pay a lot more than you would charge, and they hate their current account manager, your odds are a lot better. If your time is limited, you definitely want to prioritize working on that prospect before you work on a prospect with only one positive circumstance.

Once you have determined that the prospect is qualified, you need to explore the impact on the organization of any problems, needs, or potential special applications that you uncover. Your objective at that point is to get the prospect to agree that the problem/need exists, and that they want to fix it. Just agreeing that there is a problem is not the same as wanting to fix it.

All too often, salespeople chase after a prospect that would benefit from their product/service only to have the sale fade away with time. That usually happens because the prospect has never actually agreed that the uncovered problem is important, and that it needs to be resolved.

If a prospect agrees that there is a problem but says he has a reservation about your solution(s), do what you normally do. Ask him if he would be comfortable with whatever proof you have that verifies your claims about the benefits of your product/service, like references or technical information, etc.

However, after you provide that information, and they accept it, you have to ask again if they want to fix the problem, because in reality all they have said up to that point is that they have accepted your claim. They have not yet indicated that they are committed to using your product/service to solve the problem, and you need that commitment before you spend a lot of time on the prospect.

We will cover this issue in greater detail when we discuss strategy, but first let's discuss the information you need to get from the first meeting, information that can improve your odds of winning the account.

Actually, the information that you need could be divided into four basic categories, and there are five basic areas to explore for each category, as shown in Figure 3.1.1.

CRITICAL INFORMATION

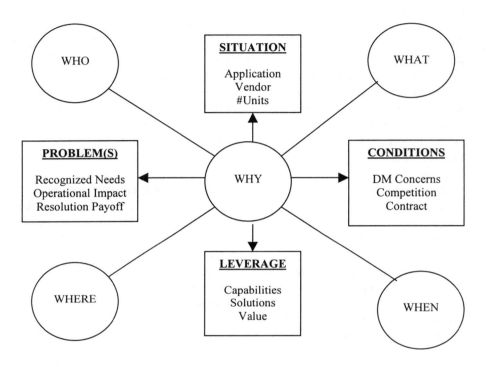

Figure 3.1.1

As you can see, the information you need in order to have a fairly comprehensive understanding of the organization's situation and needs is fairly complex. Regardless of how experienced you are, if you wing it you run the risk of forgetting to ask a key question.

Again, the best way to make sure that you don't miss any potentially critical information in the heat of the moment is to prepare a list of general questions. You can then add specific questions about their business that you pick up from research and/or from the receptionist.

Figure 3.1.2 demonstrates the specific areas and issues you need to explore in the initial meeting.

THE INVESTIGATION

	VARIABLES	ISSUES
WHAT	❖ Account dynamics ❖ Decision-maker(s) ❖ User's desires ❖ Criteria/specs	❖ How do they use your product/service? ❖ Objective(s) and concerns. ❖ Do you have any special applications? ❖ Can your company fulfill their needs?
WHO	❖ Decision-maker(s) ❖ Influencer(s) ❖ Recommender(s) ❖ Competition ❖ User(s)	❖ Are they authorized to sign? ❖ How credible are they? ❖ What level of authority? ❖ What are their capabilities, limitations, pricing? ❖ What do they need, who/what has highest priority?
WHEN	❖ Contract expiration ❖ Implement window	❖ Will you live that long? ❖ How long will it take to set up the account?
WHY	❖ Problems ❖ Weaknesses ❖ Cost reduction ❖ Increase efficiency ❖ Profit generated	❖ What solutions and benefits can you provide? ❖ Yours (compensate); competitors (leverage). ❖ For the prospect, or your employer. ❖ Same. ❖ Same.
WHERE	❖ Location(s) ❖ External interface	❖ Can your company handle their needs? ❖ What do you need to set up support?

Figure 3.1.2

In case you do not already have some type of list, the sample questions that follow should give you good start on creating one, and the case study that follows will be equally helpful. I have left out the obvious closed-ended questions, like what model, how many, etc.

SAMPLE QUESTIONS

- ➢ Tell me a little bit about your company and how you do business so that I can determine how our services might best benefit your organization.
- ➢ What types of problems are you experiencing with your current service?
- ➢ How is that affecting your organization?
- ➢ What would you like to see improved upon with your current service?
- ➢ Were you the one to make a decision to go with your current vendor?
- ➢ What made you decide to go with them?
- ➢ What would you like to change? (if you could design your own).
- ➢ What are you looking for in the company you would decide to do business with?
- ➢ Might I ask about the other vendors you are considering?
- ➢ Has there ever been a time when you needed to…, and you couldn't?
- ➢ What could it cost you in dollars not to be able to. . .?
- ➢ What happens when you cannot …? How do you handle that situation?
- ➢ Tell me how important customer service is to your business?
- ➢ Are you aware of the advantages of using…?
- ➢ What steps have you taken to update the way you use . . . in your day-to-day activities?
- ➢ What effect would better customer retention add to your bottom line?
- ➢ What does it cost you to get and keep a customer?
- ➢ How long has it been since you reevaluated your company's service?
- ➢ Why do you suppose your company has not yet taken advantage of…?

The answers to these questions/issues will enable you to figure out whether to be passionate, pass for now, or pass forever. You will also know what actions you need to take, and how long you might have to court the prospect before they fall passionately into your arms. In addition, the information will enable you to figure out the best possible strategy to leverage your sales activities for maximum effectiveness.

We will get into more detail when we get to the case study, with examples of the types of responses you might get, and how those answers would impact your sales strategy.

Finally, make sure that you take good notes during the meeting, and transfer the information to your database ASAP so that you don't forget key information. That way, you will know what you have to do and why, even if the first follow-up is six months later.

Many a sale has been lost due to lack of information, leading to premature pressure on the buyer when he is not in a position to buy. As an example, if you didn't know that someone had eight months left on his contract, you would probably start pushing him to make a decision after a couple of months, and that would obviously be the wrong strategy under the circumstances.

The right strategy in that situation would be to start with a follow-up letter, and then alternate between touch-base telephone calls and a letter or card every 60 days. That would position you to make all of your best moves to sweep him off his feet in the last months of his buying cycle. At that stage you can become indispensable if you help him develop a schedule of the steps he needs to take to avoid having problems. That way everything would be taken care of to ensure a smooth delivery, and you would be a hero.

*   *   *

TOPIC 3.1: Case Study

Scenario #1

Prospect: Association of the Romantically Deprived

Your persistence finally results in an appointment with Frank Lonelee, and you immediately start speculating as to how many pagers they have, whether they are happy..., but fortunately you are able to stop yourself, since you have several days to wait.

Then, suddenly, you are sitting in front of Frank, who turns out to be a polished professional with a great personality. You hit it off immediately. You don't see a wedding ring, and wonder if he is also a member of the Association..., but again you stop yourself. That really is more than you want to know. After the preliminary pleasantries, you explain your objectives and get his approval to proceed.

As Frank answers your first series of questions, you find out that ABC paging company currently provides the association with approximately 1,000 pagers for their various departments, and that they are pleased with the service. Naturally you are excited that they have a lot of pagers, and disappointed that the current vendor is doing a good job. The specific details are as follows:

PAGERS CURRENTLY USED

TYPE	#	EXCHANGE	COVERAGE AREA
BEEPS	50	All Local	National
DISPLAYS	750	600 Local 150 with 800 #'s	75 national 75 regional 600 local
VIBRATES	50	All Local	Local
DOES EVERYTHING	50	All 800 #'s	5 national 10 regional 35 local
AND LOOKS CUTE	100	50 Local 50 with 800 #'s	Local

USAGE DYNAMICS
- ❑ Total number currently using pagers: 1,000
- ❑ Additional units projected for 90 days: 100
- ❑ Number of units lost or destroyed over preceding year: 50
- ❑ Problems with current pagers: No spares on site
  - Missed pages in Crystal City
  - Voice mail on separate number (confusing)

FEATURES UTILIZED
- ❑ # with Group Page: 200
- ❑ # with Voice Mail : 150
- ❑ # with VibrAlert : All

I have found that designing a form to record the information that you get in the first meeting works well for me, and, since it looks official, prospects seem to be more forthcoming. If you decide to use something similar, you can easily modify the one that is included on your disk, adding as many columns and rows as you need.

If there are multiple locations, departments, or teams, I will usually fill out a separate one for each to keep the information organized. That way there is no confusion during the delivery, and my support staff can easily keep track of things.

Back to the Association. Once you have demonstrated that you are thorough, and gotten Frank into an answering mode by asking the appropriate usage questions (which also makes it easy for him to look like an expert), you move on to get information regarding the different conditions and potential leverage factors involved.

As you will see, I try to use open-ended questions as much as possible to provoke general answers that can provide the necessary information to design your strategy. The following example contains many of the basic questions you need to ask every prospect, regardless of what you sell.

THE INVESTIGATION

Q   *"What do you like most about your current paging service?"*

A   *"We can get coverage in a lot of areas, including regional and national in 100 cities."* (You can do that too, which is a great relief.)

Q   *"When you selected your current vendor, what were your criteria?"*

A   *"That they offer the coverage that we need, and system redundancy."* (Your company has back-ups, like a battery for power failures, and separate components of the transmission equipment that would instantly replace any failed counterpart.)

Q   *"What departments are using pagers currently?"*

A   *"Service, installation, security, programmers, maintenance, management."* (You make a note that service, installation, and security lead the sequence that your contact uses, which may indicate the priority of each department, so you decide to use a trick from another account, which is to tie the guard's beeper into the silent alarm system.)

Q   *"Are you aware of any particular problems that they might be experiencing?"*

A   *"We do not get any signal in our Crystal City building, but everything else seems to be fine."* (Your heart rate takes off, because you have GREAT coverage in Crystal City.)

Q   *" How does that affect the organization in terms of things like response time?"*

A   *"It is driving our cellular bills through the roof, but I 'm not sure that there has ever been a crisis as a result of the problem."* (You decide to test the waters.)

Trial Close: *"Is that something that you would want to fix?"*

A   *"I expect that the problem will be resolved pretty soon, since ABC has agreed to Install a transmitter on that building."* (You tell Frank that ABC is a good company, so they should be able to work it out. You also make a note to check with all of the department supervisors about missed pages in other areas, especially the MIS department, because a slow response to a mainframe failure could be devastating. You are a little disappointed, but not surprised that ABC is considering adding a transmitter. If it were your account, you would drive your manager crazy until it was fixed.)

Q *"I noticed from your literature that you are a national company. Do you have offices in every state?"*

A *"Yes."* (Your heart starts to beat a little faster. You think about salespeople in other branches of your company that you could call to find out if any of them have already made a sale to a branch of the association, or one of the subsidiaries, so you can pick their brains about the needs of the account. You would also love to get a good reference from the contact that your counterpart is working with.)

Q *"Where is your corporate office? Do you want them to approve the final decision?"*

A *"The corporate office is in Chicago."*

Q *"Do they typically approve the final decision?"*

A *"They usually sign off on my recommendations."* (You can determine later whether you need to make up additional proposals for someone at the corporate office, and who to address the additional copies to.)

Q *"Are there any other facilities, subsidiaries, or divisions, that might help us get you a high volume pricing break?"*

A *"As a matter of fact, we do have two subsidiaries; The Association of Lonely Porcupines, and The Association of Boring Bachelors."* (You think that this is a great lead, and if you could win either one or both of the subsidiary accounts you would be able to give a pricing break to the Association, which would make Frank look good to his boss.)

Q *"What sets your company apart from competitors?"*

A *"We are the best at bringing the lonely together."* (This point is important, because when the time is right you can stress that your company is the best in the industry as a way of avoiding the old price issue.)

Q *"Who handles your account now, an assigned account manager or the customer service department?"*

A *"The customer service department."* (Which could mean that they have no dedicated account representative, a fact that you note as a potential weakness that this particular competitor may have with other accounts. You decide to pull all of their leads that you marked with blue and approach them with a letter emphasizing the personal customer care that your customers get.)

Q   *"What is your current response time for service if your staff needs a new pager or a replacement?"*

A   *"8 hours."* (Your company has a better response time track record, so you can match or beat the incumbent vendor's response time. You casually mention it at this point, and plan to stress that fact in your proposal and capabilities summary, as well as in your approach letter to that competitor's customers.)

Q   *"How is the service currently used internally; what are the most common types of situations that occur?"*

A   *"There are some things that occur fairly frequently, like . . ."* (None of these problems sound critical, but there is one thing that you think you could leverage. You can save them the expense of some of their alphanumeric pagers by developing a coding system that eliminates the need for text messages.)

Q   *"What kind of messages usually need to be sent?"*

A   *"Usually information about which customer needs service, and the location, if it is different than the registered address."* (You plan to explore the types of problems that typically occur, and what the technician or customer service person needs to know when they talk to the customer person paging him.)

Q   *"Other than clients, who is doing the dispatching?"*

A   *"Usually supervisors and co-workers."* (You find out exactly who those people are, and write down their names so that you can interview them.)

Q   *"Where are your staff when they need to be paged?"*

A   *"Usually in their cars."* (You make a note to find out if anyone works in the basement or on extremely high floors, since the radio frequency used could affect how well the signal is capable of penetrating those areas, and you can offer an alternate frequency which is effective in any environment.)

Q   *"Who else do we need to contact for specific usage data?"*

A   *"Probably the department heads."* (You restate the ones that he had previously mentioned, and get specific extensions.)

Q   *"Does your vendor offer different services than you are currently using?"*

A   *"They also offer cellular telephones."* (You saw one of their phones, and it was from another competitor, so you need to find out why they are not getting their cellular phones from their current vendor. Frank doesn't know the answer. If the purchasing agent believes that their current vendor's phones are too expensive, you may be able to convince him/her that the pagers are also too expensive, especially in view of the value you will be adding with your excellent account support reviews and Account Support Guide.)

Q   *"Does ABC offer a national network of locations?"*

A   *"No, they are only on the eastern seaboard."* (Since the association is a national company, and the vendor that they are using locally is not able to provide service in every part of the country, you might have a distinct advantage to emphasize in your Capabilities Summary.)

BILLING

Q   *"Would you like to receive one bill for all departments, or separate bills?"*

A   *"Separate bills."* (This answer might indicate that if a problem occurred in one department, it would not affect the others, and lends added strength to your theory that you could win the account by solving the problem of the security group. It might also indicate that you would not necessarily lose the whole account if anything goes wrong with only one of the lower-priority departments, so this could represent a very long-term account.)

Q   *"Would you prefer to be billed monthly, quarterly, or annually?"*

A   *"Monthly."* (Your company offers extended period payments with a discount, so you explore their reasoning, only to find out that it is company policy not to enter into long-term vendor contracts where critical services are concerned. So, you say nothing and just forge on.)

CONCERNS

Q   *"When are you looking to change?"*

A   *"Soon."* (This would indicate some urgency, but you were hoping for a response like "as soon as possible." You now have to downgrade your projection to your supervisor. Bummer!)

Q   *"What is important to you during the transition?"*

A   *"Not having our staff miss a lot of time."* (Your competitor may have fouled up when they set up the account, causing Frank to have reservations about changing vendors. You need to emphasize your structured implementation strategy in the proposal.)

You may have noticed that, except for the first section, the questions are not exactly organized into the four categories that we discussed earlier. There are two reasons for that. To begin with, the sequence that I have used is functional, in that the questions relate to each other. The second reason is that regardless of the sequence, you never know where open-ended questions will lead your prospect. No matter how you organize your questions, you will still have to reorganize the information that you end up with into the different categories afterwards, as we will do in the next section.

I also wanted you to note the trial close that I used when the issue of problems was discussed. As I mentioned earlier, asking the prospect if a particular issue or problem is important to them, and whether they want it fixed, not just that they recognize it, is vital if you want to avoid wasting a lot of time on low-probability prospects.

You can get that type of response by asking how the problem(s) affect the organization (the impact on the organization in terms of efficiency, associated costs, and the quality of customer service), which would lead to that age-old classic, "If we could..., would you?"

If their answer is not favorable, as in the preceding example, you need to back off until you have had a chance to explore further. You can then talk to people in different departments who might be able to give you a better picture of what impact the problem is having on their departments. That way you might be able to uncover some information that your contact is not aware of, or an entirely different set of problems that you can use to leverage yourself into a winning position.

But, I digress again. Within a couple of days after your meeting, you send Frank a letter. You do not expect to make any progress with the Association in the near future, but you want to stay in touch. You make a vow that if ABC drops the ball by not installing a transmitter in Crystal City, you will figure out a romantic approach that will get every deprived person in the association beeping like crazy on your system.

TRUEBEEP CORPORATION
The paging solutions company

July 1, 1999

Mr. Frank Lee Lonelee
Association of the Romantically Deprived
6200 Love Drive
Romance, Maryland 20000

Dear Frank:

The time we spent reviewing your paging needs has been very helpful to me in understanding how you use paging to provide a total communications network.

If ABC is unable to correct the problem in Crystal City, I feel confident that Truebeep will be able to offer you a comprehensive paging service program designed to lower your total cost, while increasing the efficiency of your external paging system.

As a part of our Major Account Program, your direct paging-related responsibilities would be kept at a manageable level, beginning with a structured implementation plan. Ongoing pro-active account management will minimize problems and keep you abreast of industry and technological advances which could benefit your organization.

I look forward to working closely with you to develop a viable alternative to your current paging system if the need arises. Please contact me at (301) 555-9999 should you have any questions prior to our next meeting.

Sincerely,

Alan Salesperson
Association Paging Services Specialist

100 Vibe Boulevard . Pageheaven . Maryland . 20003 . (301) 999-6666

Frank mentioned that he had talked to Candy at PiggOut Foods and told her how great you were, and you told him that you had sent her a letter and left a couple of messages. You did not mention that you have been calling Candy every other day but only leaving an occasional message. That way you can imply that you are as busy as she is, while expressing just the right amount of interest. You don't want her to know how easily she could melt your heart.

You get a call from Candy a couple of weeks later and set an appointment to meet. Since the timing will be delayed, you decide to send her the following letter so that she won't forget you.

TRUEBEEPCORPORATION
The paging solutions company

July 2, 1999

Ms. Candy Cane
PiggOut Foods, Inc.
8000 Gourmet Plaza
Abundance, Maryland 30000

Dear Ms. Cane:

I would like to take this opportunity to confirm our appointment on October 22, 1999 at 2:00 p.m. My objective will be to find out a little about you and your company as to what your recruiting requirements involve. This will enable me to design a program for your review.

I will call to confirm our meeting and answer any preliminary questions you may have. Should your recruiting needs become top priority earlier than expected, please call me at (301) 555-9999.

Sincerely,

Alan Salesperson
Paging Services Specialist

100 Vibe Boulevard . Pageheaven . Maryland . 20003 . (301) 999-6666

Scenario #2

Prospect: NetCom

Around the same time, you also get an appointment with John Hogg at NetCom. Since you do not know that much about the high-tech industry, you stop by the NetCom office while you are in the area for another appointment and get an annual report from the receptionist so that you can do additional research.

The annual report had some interesting information that was not on their Web site, so you feel very comfortable that you will be able to talk intelligently about computer networks when you do meet with John.

During the first meeting you get the following information:

❑ As the vice president of telecommunications, John Hogg says that he is the decision-maker, but he does have to notify the CEO if the transaction value exceeds $25,000.

❑ NetCom has 3,900 service technicians, 400 of which work on-site at client facilities. The service technicians are dispatched from four regional offices, although they operate out of local offices that also house the salespeople.

❑ The technical services group has 1,800 cell phones and 400 pagers. They are currently using SlowBeep for their paging needs, and they get their phones from AllCall. The monthly expense runs about $400.00 per cell phone, and $50.00 per pager.

❑ All of the field service technicians have laptops.

❑ John admits that they have a couple of different communications problems.

1. The most frequent problem is that the installation teams communicate by email when detailed information is involved, and they sometimes have a problem finding a telephone jack on-site near their work area. As a result, they often spend too much time trying to find a free jack. They also occasionally fail to get critical information in a timely fashion if they get involved in the project; they forget to take a break to download messages.

2. The other problem involves customer response. When a customer has a problem, they contact their account support administrator, who may not be available at that moment. If the problem is critical, the customer might try to contact one of the field service engineers rather than leave a message. If that person misses a page, or is out of the cellular service area, it can be frustrating, and potentially costly to the customer.

❑   Their service agreement with SlowBeep expires in 5 months, and the agreement with AllCall has 11 months remaining.

❑   John has had a bad experience with new technology.

At this point, NetCom looks like a much better short-term prospect than the Association. You can focus on the SlowBeep agreement first, and worry about replacing some of the cellular phones later.

Since the meeting was interrupted before you got all of the information you need, you have scheduled a follow-up telephone call for next week. You decide to write down the additional questions that you are going to ask while the information is still fresh in your mind.

TOPIC 3.1: Exercise

Write down the questions that you need to ask John at NetCom when you make your follow-up call. I have completed the first couple to get you started. Think in terms of things like expense and opportunity cost (how much the company could save/earn if the problem was eliminated).

Once you have completed this exercise, you can compare your notes with the questions listed in the Appendix. The answers are also listed there.

ADDITIONAL INFORMATION NEEDED

Q Do they have any coverage problems with either pagers or cellular?

Q What is the average hourly cost of the field service staff?

Q

Q

Q

Q

Q

We will pick this up again in the next section, where you will see how the information affects your sales strategy and plan.

* * *

Appendix: Page 269
Disk: Exercise Folder

TOPIC 3.1: Assignment

Fill out the following information about one of your hot pursuits in progress:

1) Pick a mid-sized to large prospect that you have already met with but not yet proposed to, preferably one that you expect to win within 30 - 60 days.

2) Briefly explain why you picked them.

3) Fill in the answers to the list of questions from your first meeting.

4) Develop a reference list for that particular industry, including letters from your customers attesting to the "miraculous cures" that you have accomplished (or just raving about what a nice person you are).

Your Hot Pursuit

Company:

Industry:

Projected close date:

Background:

Reason you chose them:

CURRENT USAGE

TYPE	#	FEATURES	DEPARTMENT

USAGE DYNAMICS
- ❑ Total current users: _____
- ❑ Additional units projected for 90 days:_____
- ❑ Number of units lost or destroyed over preceding year:_____
- ❑ Problems with current units: _____

FEATURES UTILIZED
- ❑
- ❑
- ❑
- ❑

INVESTIGATION RESPONSES

Q Who besides your contact will be affected that you may want to involve in your presentation?

A

Q What do they like most about their current service?

A

Q When they selected their current vendor, what were their criteria?

A

Q What departments are using the product/service currently?

A

Q What problems are they experiencing?

A

Q What impact is that having on the organization in terms of efficiency, etc.?

A

Q Are there any other facilities, subsidiaries, or divisions?

A

Q Are they a national company?

A

Q Where is their corporate office? Does your contact need to get approval? From whom?

A

Q What sets their company apart from competitors?

A

Q Who handles their account now, an assigned account manager or the customer service department?

A

Q What is their current response time for service?

A

Q How is the service currently used; what are the most common types of situations that occur?

A

Q Does their vendor offer a national network of locations?
A

BILLING

Q Would they like to receive one bill for all departments, or separate bills?
A

Q Would they prefer to be billed monthly, quarterly, or annually?
A

CONCERNS

Q When are they looking to change?
A

Q What is important to your contact during the transition?
A

*   *   *

Note: If you do not have all of the information about your prospect to complete
the preceding section, you need to review the list of questions that you
use.

Disk: Assignment Folder

CHAPTER 3: Anatomy of an Effective Strategy

TOPIC 3.2: Developing a Sales Strategy and Action Plan

SKILLSET TOPIC(S)
❑   Identifying conditions and leverage issues
❑   Understanding the planning process
❑   Integrating the key elements into a sales strategy
❑   Developing an effective action plan

OBJECTIVE
To provide a vehicle for you to use information from the first meeting to develop a game plan that will give you an advantage over your competitors and increase your odds of winning the account.

BENEFITS
✓   Integrate all of the critical elements of the purchasing process into your sales strategies.
✓   Relate your action plans to the specific account dynamics more effectively.
✓   Present the appropriate solutions to any problems and conditions, while leveraging your advantages.
✓   Address the needs/wants of each decision-maker.
✓   Prioritize your sales activities more efficiently.
✓   Orchestrate your sales steps to fully coincide with the prospect's buying cycle.

> "All of the conditions/ variables that might impede the sales process need to be addressed in your strategy, while your plan times the steps that bypass or resolve those issues to coincide with your prospect's buying cycle."

I don't know about you, but when I think I have a good shot at winning the account, different parts of the conversation that we had will keep replaying in my mind long after that first meeting.

That is not a bad thing. The fact is, you need to think about the information you picked up in the first meeting while it is fresh in your mind so that you can address the key elements in your strategy. That way, your plan will resolve or bypass any conditions that could block the sale.

Of course, you also have to time the steps of your plan to coincide with the buying cycle of your prospect, not your quota deadline. I strongly recommend that you write out your strategy and plan instead of winging it to ensure that you don't forget an important step, especially when the sale drags on for months.

I jot mine down on a page in my planner after the meeting, unless I know it is going to take a while, at which point I will break down and write something formal for their file. To be honest, I learned that lesson the hard way. I once lost a really huge sale because, thinking that the sale would only take a month to close, I thought out a strategy and proceeded to implement my brilliant plan without writing anything down.

In fact, the sale took eight months to close due to the unexpected merger of two different divisions. After I had presented the proposal, which I had prepared eight months earlier, my contact told me that they had decided to go with one of my competitors. I was heartbroken. I figured that I would have to sell the island that I had bought, populated only with members of the opposite...

I had enough presence of mind to ask why, and then I became REALLY depressed. She told me that one of our references complained about poor support. I had made a mental note to verify my references back when I included them in the proposal, but without having any notes to remind me eight months later, I blew it.

Forgetting a key element of your sales plan is irrelevant, however, if your plan itself is flawed. In order to put a good plan together, you start with the information from the first meeting.

As you will recall, that information consists of the four categories listed in Figure 3.2.1.

CRITICAL INFORMATION

(Proposal
and
Presentation)

THE SITUATION:
What/who they currently use, how many units, how it is working, the positive aspects the DM likes, etc.

THE PROBLEM:
The impact on the organization in terms of efficiency, associated costs, and the quality of customer service.

CONDITIONS:
What concerns the DM has, who are your competitors, what is the contractual situation.

LEVERAGE:
What you can do better, or differently, to help them increase efficiency, reduce costs, etc.

(Strategy
and
Action Plan)

Figure 3.2.1

While all of the information you get from the first meeting will affect your strategy, the situational information is primarily used to design the system or program that you ultimately recommend, and to develop your pricing strategy, both of which will become the foundation of your proposal. The solutions to the problems that you uncover are an important part of the proposal, but they should also become the key components of your presentation.

The other two categories, conditions that you have to resolve before the sale can be consummated and potential leverage areas that you can use to improve your odds of winning the account, become the key elements of your strategy.

After you have developed your strategy, you can figure out the specific steps that you need to take to resolve those conditions, and leverage your advantages. Those steps will become the sales plan. Once you have figured out what steps to take, you can assign a priority to each step and plan the timing, which would obviously be directly related to the anticipated length of the prospect's buying cycle.

The result represents your action plan: what you are going to do, and when, to win the sale. Thus, your sales plan is merely a series of actions/events that are a direct result of your sales strategy, as demonstrated in Table 3.2.2.

PLANNING PROCESS

Analyze Conditions/Variables	Identify Leverage Areas
❑ **Like:** they're under contract.	❑ **Like:** your special billing system.
Add Solution(s) to Strategy	**Factor Leverage Into Strategy**
❑ **Like:** penetrate another division first, promoting the billing system, and come back to primary contract 30 days before contract review (60 days before renewal).	❑ **Like:** find out what their billing system weaknesses are, and extend the capabilities section in the proposal for their sales group (normally one page, go to two pages, which you already did for World Bank; you just copy it).
Develop Pricing/Proposal	**Develop an Action Plan**
❑ Based on current vendor and/or competitor(s).	❑ Schedule when to penetrate another division, etc.

Table 3.2.2

Now that we have reviewed the process, we can take an in-depth look at each of the components, beginning with:

THE ELEMENTS OF YOUR STRATEGY

We have already discussed most of the conditions that you will run into, like delayed purchase decisions, multiple competitors, spreadsheet bid reviews, and the highly efficient multilevel decision-making approval process (not). Before we look at the detailed analysis that you would typically use to reach those conclusions, let's review the possible leverage areas that you might be able to use to resolve the conditions, concerns, and objections that your prospects may or may not state.

Any reason why a prospect should consider doing business with your company instead of their current vendor, such as ridiculous savings, is a leverage point. The solutions and benefits that your future client will get are also leverage areas, as are weaknesses in your competitor's position.

Your competitor's weaknesses can be a powerful tool to leverage the value of your product/service, but you want to emphasize your company's strength in those areas rather than bad-mouthing your competitor. Your list of leverage issues might also include something as intangible as the priority level your contact has assigned to a particular department; if you can satisfy their needs better than the incumbent vendor or the competition.

Even your understanding of a particular company's buying cycle could represent a significant advantage or leverage area. Your competitors might be inexperienced and try to push the decision through faster, even though the existing conditions make that impossible, while your sales steps would conform to the buying cycle of your intended.

Figure 3.2.3 lists some of the different conditions that will affect your success in selling to a prospect, and the leverage issues that you can use to enhance your position, and perhaps influence those conditions.

SALES STRATEGY ISSUES

POTENTIAL CONDITIONS	POSSIBLE LEVERAGE AREAS
❑ Budget constraints	✓ Your pricing and ROI
❑ Buyer's concerns/preconceived ideas	✓ Your references and proven successful applications
❑ Buyer's level of sophistication	✓ Your professionalism, and sales tools
❑ Contractual obligation	✓ The quality and timing of your sales steps
❑ Needs of the organization	✓ Your solutions and benefits
❑ Competition	✓ Your strengths/competitor's weaknesses
❑ Contact's desires	✓ Identified "hot buttons" you can push

Figure 3.2.3

I hate to add this, but there is another significant variable that you need to factor into your strategy. The role of your contact in the organization will seriously affect your ability to make the sale, as well as the length of the process. While you want to present to the final decision-maker or someone in upper management, like a vice president (refer to the Organizational Structure table, Figure 2.3.2 on Page 41), that is not always practical in very large companies.

Fortunately, any contact can provide you with the information that you need and help you win the account, once you figure out his role in the organization. If they are qualified to impact the decision, your contact will probably fit into one of several roles, and most will have a combination of two or more, like being a user of your product or service, and perhaps an influencer.

When someone is fulfilling multiple roles within the organization you can appeal to all of those roles, as you can see in Figure 3.2.4.

CONTACT ANALYSIS

TITLE/ROLE	LEVEL OF AUTHORITY/ FUNCTION
DECISION-MAKER	Individual responsible for, or authorized to make, the final decision (while you want to try for the CEO, a vice president, or a director, a line manager is often empowered to sign for certain types of transactions. Of course, it is always good to be referred by the CEO, etc.).
RECOMMENDER	Individual who recommends the vendor of choice and has the responsibility of presenting their selection to the final decision-maker. This person is usually a manager.
INFLUENCER	Individual who can help you position yourself with either the recommender or decision-maker. Could be anyone from a vice president to a well-connected executive secretary.
SCREENER	Individual authorized to investigate vendors by gathering information to submit to the next person in the chain of command. While this individual is usually a manager, it could just as easily be a secretary, and they might also be the recommender or influencer.
PURCHASING	Individual responsible for evaluating vendors and internal requests for new products or services for the organization. This person is frequently not the final decision-maker.
END-USER	May be the department head, or the actual end user, and is sometimes also a recommender or influencer.

Figure 3.2.4

Clearly, the role of your contact in the formal and informal organizational structure is significant. You need to factor that issue into your strategy. If they have to get approval from another party, you need to help them sell it to the next person in the chain with hard facts and a professional proposal. Your contact's role will also often affect the length of the sales process.

The sad truth is that many managers in very large companies are not authorized to sign for toilet paper without somebody else looking over their shoulder. It might only be a rubber stamp ritual, but that approval procedure will usually delay the process.

It has been my experience that the greater the amount of money being spent, the more decision-makers involved, so don't be surprised if it takes longer than your contact expects when they are not the final decision-maker.

Aside from the issue of how much influence they have, the role of your contact in the organization will also affect your strategy in a different way.

While all of your prospects are going to be somewhat concerned with general issues that relate to the decision, like price and quality, they will also have specific concerns and hot buttons based on their role in the company.

As an example, an end user of any product or service will usually be more concerned with how that product or service works than about the price. On the other hand, the purchasing agent in an organization is usually most concerned with how your purchase price compares to others, and they tend to be experts at spreadsheet comparison and evaluation.

An accountant might be very concerned about billing issues, and is typically harder to pencil sell (Return on Investment calculation). Since they tend to be analytical, you need to have your facts straight, and it helps if they provide the figures.

If you were dealing with the comptroller of an organization, he/she would be interested in exploring the difference between purchasing and leasing your product or service. You want to present information about how long the payback would take, and discuss the tax implications of each choice. You would definitely want the comptroller to help you develop the numbers that you use to calculate ROI.

While the final decision-maker would be concerned about all aspects of the transaction to some degree, they would be more likely to base the final decision upon whether or not they like you, if all other factors between you and your competitors are basically equal. On the other hand, the accountant in an organization would probably be much less likely to make an emotional decision.

Let's analyze the role of your contact in the first scenario of the case study to determine how it would affect your approach based on the examples that we have reviewed.

You know that Frank is not the final decision-maker because he has to get approval from corporate. He is probably a recommender, and may be an influencer, so when you present your proposal it would make sense to prepare a second copy for him to give to his supervisor. When you develop your strategy for the Association of the Romantically Deprived, you would want to stress how easy it will be for Frank to manage the new system as a result of your terrific account support.

Because he is an end user, you would probably also want to enthusiastically rave about the capabilities of your network and products (end users love new toys). Finally, you will want to pencil sell him as to the great deal that he is going to get, but you don't need to have him provide the numbers unless he happens to be very analytical.

That basically describes how the role of your contact in the purchasing process, and his/her level of authority, will determine how you approach the sale, what areas you need to emphasize, and how you need to present your information.

As you know, people often buy what they want, not necessarily just what they need. You can usually determine what their specific hot buttons (wants) are by identifying their role(s), instead of just addressing their needs. Understanding your contact(s)' role and hot buttons is also essential when you do your presentation.

That knowledge will enable you to assign the appropriate priority to the order in which you present your solutions and leverage points, and the detail with which you describe each, based on what is most important to your contact. Needless to say, the problem that your contact told you he/she wanted to fix will always be on the top of the list of advantages that you discuss.

Finally, in addition to the chain of command that you are actively working on, the users and supervisors might need to be considered and influenced, depending on your product or service. Get their feedback, and take the time to win them over because they will sometimes be able to tell you what the real problems are, why, and how to solve them.

Now let's look at how you actually develop the strategy based on the types of variables that we have covered. Table 3.2.5 demonstrates how you might address each issue.

SALES STRATEGY

ISSUES TO RESOLVE	POSSIBLE ACTIONS
❏ **DECISION-MAKER'S CONCERNS** ✓ Credibility of your company. ✓ Your contact is afraid that your system does not cover part of the territory.	❏ **PEACE-OF-MIND MEASURES** ✓ Provide references and annual report. ✓ Have his drivers test coverage. ✓ Get map of competitor's coverage.
❏ **CONDITION** ✓ They need totally failsafe system performance.	❏ **SOLUTION** ✓ Bring your engineer to the next meeting to discuss your failsafe back-up system.
❏ **SUPPORT** ✓ The original implementation by their current vendor was a disaster.	❏ **TECHNIQUE** ✓ Set up an implementation meeting to plan the transition, and send a memo to all department heads.

Table 3.2.5

The steps that result from your strategy become your objectives, which you simply prioritize and assign a completion date. Almost all of your steps or actions will have to be accomplished in a certain sequence to ensure winning the account, which is why you have to assign specific or relative dates to each step.

Since those factors could change, you should also be prepared to use an alternative strategy if necessary. (This process will become automatic as you draw from your experiences.)

Putting all of your objectives, the factors that will affect the sale, and alternatives that increase your odds of winning the sale into an outline helps you focus in on any vulnerable areas and keep track of where you are in the sales cycle. It will also help you to determine the priority level of each objective/action based on when they might close. The planning process is as follows:

ACTION PLANNING

TYPICAL OBJECTIVES/ACTIONS

> ➤ Issue proposal by/on 6/28.
> ➤ Provide sample to John Smith by/on 7/1.
> ➤ Meet with users to define problems/gather input by 7/10.
> ➤ Confirm that your product/service will perform (testing) by 7/12.
> ➤ Get internal approval for offer on 7/5.
> ➤ Sign contract on/by 7/15.

FACTORS WHICH MIGHT CHANGE

> ➤ Change in client evaluation criteria or specification.
> ➤ New competitor submits bid.
> ➤ Deprioritization of project.
> ➤ Decision-maker is promoted or quits.
> ➤ Merger, acquisition, or reorganization.

ALTERNATIVE ACTIONS

> ➤ Get partial order or abandon.
> ➤ Go over your contact's head.
> ➤ Put on ice and begin follow-up campaign.

The timing of your sales plan is just as important as the steps themselves, just like the timing of any plan. As you can see from the table that follows, all action plans consist of a series of interlocking steps, and they typically have to follow a certain sequence.

In fact, a sales plan is really no different than a plan to seduce the love of your life. In both cases, various activities have to be coordinated so that they follow one another, with each of the various phases synchronized to facilitate the next one:

STEPS TO THE SEDUCTION	STEPS TO THE SALE
❑ *Lay awake at night.* ❑ *Take cold showers.* ❑ *Brainstorm strategy.* ❑ *Get more information from friends.* ❑ *Set up date.* ❑ *Book reservations at their favorite restaurant.* ❑ *Pick up bottle of their favorite wine.* ❑ *Read up on their favorite topic?* ❑ *Get haircut, manicure.* ❑ *Buy new outfit.* ❑ *Clean and wax car.* ❑ *Pick up or meet date.* ❑ *Pray!!!*	▪ Brainstorm strategy. ▪ Develop Action Chart. ▪ Set up meeting with user(s). ▪ Get more information from your contact. ▪ Develop pricing. ▪ Call the salesperson handling another branch of the prospective company, perhaps in another state. ▪ Set up demonstration. ▪ Review competitor information, and determine strengths and weaknesses. ▪ Send letter outlining previous meeting and develop proposal. ▪ Set meeting to present proposal/negotiate. ▪ Set meeting to get order, review account management, and set up an implementation meeting.

Clearly, any plan involves taking certain key steps scheduled in a specific sequence. While you might have some flexibility as to the sequence, missing one or more of those steps could lower your odds in either case.

For instance, if you skipped asking friends about a person's likes and dislikes in the process of planning a seduction, you might pick the wrong restaurant. That might not be critical, but it would lower your odds a bit. In sales, making mistakes or using bad timing when you are pursuing a prospect is a lot more critical. It would cause you to lose potential commissions when you fail to win an account, and you also lose all potential add-on sales, as well as referrals. Not good!

In summary, you can win a higher percentage of the major accounts you pursue if you take effective actions to influence the factors that will affect your ability to win the account. You find out what variables are involved in the first meeting, and use that information to develop your strategy (the actions you need to take), which will become part of your action plan. When you consider your plan you have to view the sales process as a series of actions that you have to take in order to successfully win the account.

Again, the issues that determine your actions are conditions that you have to work around or resolve, and leverage areas, which are advantages you can use to improve your position relative to your competition. You determine what those actions/sales steps should be when you develop your strategy to deal with the issues that will impact your ability to achieve your objective. While some steps might be interchangeable, others would have to be completed before the next step could possibly take place.

Your sales plan would include some of the same steps for every situation, plus different steps based on each different set of variables involved. Even when you use the same strategy for two different sales situations, the individual sales steps will usually have to be timed differently for each, depending on what time frame the decision making process will span. The longest sales cycle usually occurs when you initiate a company's buying cycle, but could also be the result of some major change like an acquisition, a reorganization, or even a hostile takeover.

Needless to say, when you develop a strategy for a prospect with a long buying cycle, in addition to resolving any conditions and concerns, you also have to keep your relationship with the decision-maker(s) alive until they are in a position to make a decision. That usually involves adding several steps to your normal sales process, some of which could be eliminated if the sales cycle compresses for some reason, or if other, more critical prospects require your attention.

While a long selling cycle might seem like a major pain, there are some advantages.

❑ You will have time to do research on the company and possibly the industry, if necessary.

❑ Your contact in the company will become a lot more comfortable with you, which will give you an edge over salespeople who come to bid later in the buying cycle.

❑ If the incumbent vendor drops the ball, you will be in position to take over the account earlier than expected.

❑ You will have time to brainstorm additional issues that need to be factored into your strategy.

You can use the blank forms that follow in the case study to outline your own strategy for each new breathless experience that you work on. Refer to the case study to guide you in developing those strategies.

Keep a record of each creative solution that you come up with when you run into a critical problem while working with one of your prospects or customers. Those solutions will come in handy when you run into a similar situation in the future. Using everything you do as the building block for future actions is a very efficient way to grow as a professional.

In my opinion, starting from scratch each time is like operating in the Stone Age. There is nothing wrong with it, except that cavemen were the absolute worst salespeople. (They didn't do too well romantically, either, since they had to beat their intended over the head with a club to get a date.)

* * *

TOPIC 3.2: Case Study

Scenario #1

Prospect: Association of the Romantically Deprived

Meanwhile, back at the ranch…soon after your initial meeting with Frank you found out that ABC Company agreed to put up a transmitter in the weak area, and Frank has decided to stick with them. You told Frank that you respected him for being loyal to his account manager in spite of their delay in resolving the problem. You don't think that he could hear you crying, because you put your hand over the phone when you couldn't stifle the occasional sob.

Actually, you are not totally devastated because their contract still has four months to run, and you will have an earlier shot if ABC fails to perform. Even if ABC installs the transmitter, you decide that it would still be worth pursuing, although you would give it a lower priority. Even though they like the incumbent salesperson, you do have some leverage. You have an edge in pricing and can offer a national network to differentiate yourself from ABC.

Even better, their current vendor has made some serious mistakes. Even if they solve the problem of missed pages by putting up a new transmitter, they lost some credibility by reacting too slowly, which is the only reason why Frank talked to you in the first place.

Besides, now that you know that the association uses around 1,000 pagers, which would represent six months' quota for you, you think that you may be in lust. Since you have made the decision to pursue whether or not ABC drops the ball again, you have to develop a plan as to how you will accomplish that objective, so with a heavy sigh, you get started.

THE SEDUCTION

STEP #1

Organize the information from the first meeting.

CRITICAL INFORMATION
Price/Proposal

THE SITUATION	THE PROBLEM
☐ They have 1,000 pagers in service (refer to Current Usage).	✓ Unfortunately, the only real problem at the moment seems to be poor coverage in Crystal City.
☐ The departments are service, site security, installation, programming, maintenance, and management.	✓ A potential problem might be in the making if ABC keeps dragging their feet about putting a transmitter in Crystal City.
☐ They are a national company with two subsidiaries (you don't know who the subs are using, # pagers, etc.).	✓ They are using expensive alphanumeric pagers for some applications where less expensive digital pagers would work with a coding system.
☐ Users get most pages in their cars.	
☐ ABC subcontracts their nationwide pagers (they do not own a nationwide network).	✓ You don't really have Frank's commitment to make a change, but he seems to like you. After all, he did refer you to Candy.
☐ It is company policy not to enter into any long-term contracts for critical services.	

Once you have classified the situational and problem related information, that information will help you develop your strategy and enable you to work on getting pricing approved. When the time is right, it will also provide you with the basic information you need to develop your proposal.

Your next step is to summarize the conditions and leverage information, to make sure that you address the key variables that will affect the sales process in your basic strategy.

CRITICAL INFORMATION
Strategy/Plan

CONDITIONS	LEVERAGE
❑ Contract expires in 4 months (or 60 days, if ABC company fails to install a transmitter in Crystal City). Should deprioritize if ABC installs the transmitter as promised.	✓ Acceptable chemistry.
❑ Mr. Lonelee is an influencer, not the final DM.	✓ You can satisfy needs/wants and have a good match if your system has strong Crystal City coverage.
❑ DM is concerned with coverage and system fail-safe.	✓ Reasonable price advantage.
❑ Need to meet with department heads to get actual unit count.	✓ You have a great system with total redundant backup.
❑ They are happy with ABC, but that could change if ABC keeps dragging its feet about putting in a transmitter in Crystal City.	✓ At least one of the department heads really likes your system features.
	✓ You started their buying cycle, so there will be fewer competitors (you hope).

STEP #2

How well you do at this point will directly affect your pricing, because the better your strategy, the less you will have to discount.

PROFILE

DATE: 3/11/99
PROJECT: Association of the Romantically Deprived
BUYING CYCLE: Might be four months
SALES PROCESS: 3 - 5 sales calls
ACCOUNT VOLUME: Very Large

OBJECTIVES	Position yourself to participate in the bidding process when their contract comes up for renewal in July 1999, or sooner if their current contract is breached (you wish!).
STRATEGY	Keep in touch just in case ABC Paging fails to install a transmitter in the weak coverage area (and reconfirm that your system has good coverage in that area).
	Identify any other local user groups in the association that are not under the same contract, even if they only use two pagers (if you have a good internal reference when you go to bid, it would help).
	Identify any other chapters of the association that use your company's system, and talk to their account manager to find out about any special uses for their pagers.
CLASSIFICATION	You hope that it will turn into a quickie, but are prepared to take a cold shower or two if ABC installs a new transmitter.
PROGNOSIS	Clearly merits developing an action plan, but you want to prioritize it for action after current quickies.
	If ABC installs a transmitter you will need to reprioritize it by sending form letters and touching base by phone occasionally until about 60 days before their contract expires.

STEP #3

After you select the solutions and most significant leverage areas to emphasize, you can determine what steps you need to take to satisfy their needs and leverage your advantages.

In order to be effective, you need to make sure that you cover every base with the steps in your action plan, taking into account all of the conditions and issues that you need to deal with. I also strongly recommend that you write out your action plan so that you don't miss anything, especially if the sales cycle might span a long period of time, like several months.

In this particular case there is no urgency, except that you want to be in position to move quickly if ABC Paging fails to install the transmitter.

Your Action Plan

ACTION	DATE
■ File for 60 day follow-up.	
■ Close security division for 14 pagers.	→ ASAP
■ Test beeper when in ABC's weak area.	→ When in area
■ Call to see if ABC installed a transmitter.	→ 4/11
■ Call other ABC customers in weak area (highlighting the top edge of your cards comes in handy now).	→ Immediately
■ Send paging frequency performance analysis.	→ 4/20
■ Call other major account salespeople to find out if they have an account with any association branches to learn more about needs; get references.	
■ Look up SIC code to see if your local branch has any similar account applications: any special things their accounts use.	→ 4/20
■ Call for survey appointment to develop bid/contract review.	→ 6/1
	→ 6/15
■ Develop proposal/present.	→ 6/30
	→ 7/1
■ Send tie-line feasibility study.	→ 7/15
■ Conduct Implementation meeting/deliver.	

Possible Alternative Actions:
❑ Reprioritize if ABC installs transmitter.

MODULE 3.2: Exercise

❏ Now you get a chance to work out a strategy and sales plan for NetCom based on the information that we covered in the investigation. Once you have completed this exercise on the disk, you can refer to the Appendix to verify your answers.

1) Review the variables that could impact your ability to win the account.

2) Fill out a profile.

3) Complete your action plan.

STEP #1

CRITICAL INFORMATION
Price/Proposal

THE SITUATION

❑ The technical services group has 1,800 cell phones and 400 pagers; sales group has 150 units combined.

❑ They use SlowBeep for their pagers, and AllCall for cellular phones.

❑ Their average monthly cost is $400 per phone, and $50 per pager.

❑ All of the field techs have laptops.

❑ Their contract with SlowBeep expires in 5 months, and the AllCall agreement expires in 11 months.

❑ The average hourly cost of techs is $40, billing is $150 per hour, and they bill a client an average of $80,000 per year.

THE PROBLEM

✓ The installation teams sometimes have a problem finding a telephone jack on-site near their work area, so they spend too much time trying to find a free jack.

✓ They occasionally fail to get critical information in a timely fashion if they get involved in the project; they forget to take a break to download messages.

✓ When a customer has a critical problem and their support administrator is not available, they try to contact the field service engineers. If that person misses a page or is out of the cellular service area, it can be frustrating and potentially costly to the customer.

CRITICAL INFORMATION
Strategy/Plan

CONDITIONS

❑ The primary contract expires in 5 months, and the secondary contract expires in 11 months, so you need to focus on the primary.

❑ Your two-way pagers are more expensive than SlowBeep's regular units, so you need to concentrate on showing John how much NetCom will save in lost time.

❑ John is a DM, but the value of your service exceeds $25,000, so John will have to pass it by the CEO.

❑ John is concerned with system reliability, and he has had a bad experience with new technology.

❑ The current vendor has had the account for over 5 years, and has probably built up some loyalties.

❑ It is NetCom policy to review at least three bids.

❑ John has not fully committed to making the change, even if your system fulfills the promise that you have made.

LEVERAGE

✓ Your contact at the World Bank plays golf with John, so you should be able to get some insight about John.

✓ You can improve efficiency and eliminate the current problems, and the value of the efficiency savings alone will more than make up the difference in price.

✓ You have a great proposal that you will duplicate so that John can forward it to the CEO.

✓ You have a great system with total system backup.

✓ The current vendor has limited text capabilities and no plans to expand it.

✓ No other vendor offers the data packet capabilities of your system.

✓ If the CEO sees the payback numbers (ROI calculations, covered in the next chapter), he will probably at least approve units for the team leaders.

STEP #2

PROFILE

DATE: 5/2/99
PROJECT: NetCom
BUYING CYCLE: 5 months for primary, 11 months for secondary
SALES CYCLE: 5 - 8 sales calls
ACCOUNT VOLUME: Very Large

OBJECTIVES

STRATEGY

CLASSIFICATION

PROGNOSIS

Appendix: Page 270
Disk: Exercise Folder

STEP #3

Put together an action plan. You can skip the exact dates of each action because that is not as important as the sequence of events.

Your Action Plan

ACTION	DATE
▪	
▪	
▪	
▪	
▪	
▪	
▪	
▪	
▪	
▪	
▪	
▪	
▪	
▪	
▪	
▪	

Possible Alternative Actions:

Appendix: Page 271
Disk: Exercise Folder

MODULE 3.2: Assignment

1) List the variables involved that will impact your ability to win your own prospect-in-progress.

2) Fill out a profile.

3) Complete your action plan.

STEP #1

Recap the basic information you have accumulated up to this point.

CRITICAL INFORMATION
Price/Proposal

THE SITUATION	THE PROBLEM
❑	✓
❑	✓
❑	✓
❑	✓
❑	✓
❑	✓

Disk: Assignment Folder

CRITICAL INFORMATION
Strategy/Plan

CONDITIONS	LEVERAGE
❑	✓
❑	✓
❑	✓
❑	✓
❑	✓
❑	✓
❑	✓
❑	✓

Disk: Assignment Folder

STEP #2

PROFILE

DATE:
PROJECT:
BUYING CYCLE:
SALES CYCLE:
ACCOUNT VOLUME:

OBJECTIVES	
STRATEGY	
CLASSIFICATION	
PROGNOSIS	

STEP #3

Your Action Plan

ACTION	DATE
▪	
▪	
▪	
▪	
▪	
▪	
▪	
▪	
▪	
▪	
▪	
▪	
▪	
▪	
▪	

Possible Alternative Actions:

Disc: Assignment Folder

CHAPTER FOUR

A Winning Proposition

"Moving the relationship to the next plateau is always a delicate balancing act. On the one hand, you want to make sure that they are ready to buy before you ask, but on the other hand you also want to make the sale before you die of old age."

CHAPTER 4: A Winning Proposition

TOPIC 4.1: Sales Forecasting

SKILLSET TOPIC(s)
❑ Using a sales cycle flow chart
❑ Maintaining a Pipeline Report

OBJECTIVE
To help you more accurately forecast the window of time when you expect to book the business by using a pipeline system.

BENEFITS
✓ Take the stress out of forecasting.
✓ Forecast more accurately.
✓ Plan your productivity to avoid dry spells.
✓ Time your productivity to take advantage of contests and bonuses.

> "If you don't really have any kind of system, forecasting may seem sort of like picking horses at the track, often with about the same results."

I want to briefly address the process of sales forecasting, and I figured that this might be good place to do it. If you are like most salespeople I know, predicting which accounts you expect to win is not an exact science. You may change your mind a dozen times before you project your numbers, and even then you might have lingering doubts.

My analysis process used to go something like: "Yes, they will close... well, maybe they will... actually, come to think about it, they probably won't... but I am going to put it down anyway because I really don't have much going for this month, and besides, something could change! Let us pray."

When you stop to think about it, isn't that sort of like picking horses at the track? Some of my picks are still trying to get to the finish line. Being wrong when you estimate the closing dates on your pending prospects wouldn't be a problem if your manager had a sense of humor, but none of mine ever seemed amused when my projections fell way short.

In fact, until I learned how to forecast more effectively, I used to think that it was ridiculous when, at the beginning of each month, my manager would ask me to forecast which sales I was going to close that month. After all, if I knew who was going to buy from me in advance, I wouldn't have to run around talking to tons of people, just the ones who were going to buy.

As you have probably already guessed, I still talk to a lot of people, and not all of them end up buying from me. Now, however, I am a lot better at deciding who will probably decide to choose my company, and when that happy event will likely take place.

Estimating the probability and timing of the sale can be challenging, but there is a fairly effective system you can use to avoid the problem of high or low projections. I learned this particular method from one of my managers (under threat of death by strangulation).

You start by looking at how qualified the prospect is, as we discussed earlier. To recap, if a company is getting bids, they are certainly qualified. However, if they are getting bids and having problems with billing, your odds become a little bit better because they are more likely to make a change. When a prospect has more than two positive indicators – they are shopping for a new vendor, they currently pay a lot more than your company would charge, and they hate their current account manager – your odds are a lot better.

If your contact agrees that the problem/need that you are addressing exists, and that they want to fix it, your odds take a quantum leap. If they just agree that there is a problem without a commitment, you need to factor in the different conditions that will affect the sale and the leverage areas that you can use to positively influence those conditions. The more leverage areas you identify that you will be able to use in the sales process, the more your odds increase, as demonstrated in Table 4.1.1.

INFLUENCIAL ISSUES

CONDITIONS	LEVERAGE ISSUES
❏ Number of competitors involved.	✓ Your sales strategy and action plan.
❏ Decision-maker's concerns.	✓ The quality of your presentation of your company's capabilities.
❏ Buyer's level of sophistication.	✓ Your level of professionalism, and the sales tools that you use.
❏ Long buying cycles.	✓ The quality and timing of your sales steps.
❏ Intricate needs configuration.	✓ Your needs analysis and the resulting recommendation(s).
❏ Professionalism of competitors.	✓ The level of value/trust that you have established
❏ Contact's level of influence.	✓ Identified hot buttons you can push.

Table 4.1.1

Evaluating the conditions you face, and any leverage you might have, will help you determine which bids you have a high probability of winning with more accuracy. But if they have no deadline to make the decision, it does not help you figure out when they will take delivery.

Fortunately, accurate forecasting when there is no deadline is not that tough if you look at the right variables. Table 4.1.2 contains a flow chart that demonstrates the likely probability of your winning an account based on the stage of the sales cycle. To ensure more accurate forecasts, you simply look at the stage of the sales process that you have completed, and then factor in your closing ratio. I'm sure you would agree that, at best, you have about a 50% chance of winning an account that you are about to propose to. If you are meeting to review an implementation strategy, however, your probability is substantially higher.

FORECAST FLOW CHART

POINT IN SALES CYCLE	ODDS
Begin ritual by calling/stopping by	5%
First date (if they are qualified)	20%
Sales strategy brainstorm	40%
Develop proposal	45%
Presentation	50%
Start pipeline/forecasting	50%
Negotiate	60%
Develop implementation strategy/manual	70%
Implementation meeting	80%

Table 4.1.2

Even if you have 30 accounts you are working on but have only proposed to 10 who expect to make a decision within 30 days, your forecast should involve only those 10, and it would be based on your closing ratio. However, if the majority of them are well past the proposal point and closer to the end of their sales cycles, you could use a higher closing percentage. I say that because some of the less likely prospects have probably already been discarded.

I always leave a safety margin in case something goes wrong. After all, how many cold showers have you had to take over the years when your romantic expectations were a bit premature?

In addition to using the flow chart, the way to get the most accurate projection of when an account will actually be delivered is to set up an implementation timeline. You establish an event timeline by working with the client to schedule the things that have to be done in a given sequence to ensure a smooth delivery. That way, you know exactly when you are going to deliver, and you have time to make sure that everything is in place.

Don't forget that unless your contact has final approval authority, he/she may not have total control over when the purchase is approved, so you should still develop a contingency plan in case there is a delay.

The final key to making the process accurate when you start juggling a lot of different affairs is an organized format for quick tracking and reporting purposes. You can easily resolve that problem by listing your prospects on a tracking sheet. If you are not already using some type of form or tool for forecasting, or if one you are using does not always work well, you might want to consider using the same one I use, which is called a "Pipeline Report." It works pretty well, and it is easy to design.

There are basically two key sections. The first section contains "short-timers" that will make the decision within 30 days. If you have $100,000 potential in this section, and your closing ratio is 40%, you would project $40,000 for the month. The second section contains prospects that you expect to close within 60 to 90 days. You need to develop at least as many prospects for this section as you have in the 30-day section, because they will replace the ones you win or lose each month.

This section is just as important as the first section. It allows you to control productivity by giving you advance warning when you have too few new prospects working to replace the current month's sales and those that you lose. If you know that you will run dry before you even start the new month, you can start pumping in some new prospects at the beginning of the month instead of panicking near the end of the month and having to lie to your sales manager . . . again.

A forecast tracking sheet can be a terrific tool to help you balance your income and keep your direct supervisor happy, as long as you keep your pipeline filled with romantic possibilities. In conclusion, managing your pipeline can help you avoid entering that uncomfortable "Dry Zone" (which occasionally precedes the even worse "Poverty Zone").

* * *

TOPIC 4.1: Case Study

Scenario #1

Prospect: Association of the Romantically Deprived

Speaking of forecasting, things with the Association are moving slower than molasses running down an icicle. . . well, you get the general idea.

Since you have a bit of spare time, you send the following message in response to a recent conversation during which Frank mentioned that he understands very little about the different paging radio frequencies.

While every vendor claims that their particular product or service is the best, few will go to the extra lengths that you will to prove it. Don't forget that you are also trying to kill time until he is ready to review your offer.

This could be your "Letter #16" for future prospects that you need to stay in touch with over a long period.

TRUEBEEPCORPORATION
The paging solutions company

July 8, 1999

Mr. Frank Lee Lonelee
Association of the Romantically Deprived
6200 Love Drive
Romance, Maryland 20000

Dear Frank:

I have enclosed some information regarding paging frequencies for your review. I hope the attached pages put the information into perspective as you review vendor proposals.

The Ultra High Frequency band that you will be using with Truebeep pagers (912.3456 Mhz) offers excellent building penetration. The multiplicity of transmitting towers and height of transmitters will compensate for the limited range of the UHF signal, thereby providing extended area coverage in addition to excellent penetration.

Please feel free to call me at any time if I can be of any further assistance.

Sincerely,

Alan Salesperson
Association Paging Services Specialist

Enclosure
AS/twp

PAGING FREQUENCY ANALYSIS

RANGE AND PENETRATION

The table below describes the different available frequency bands and their associated characteristics. When you begin your paging capability review, this will help you match the different systems that you are considering to most closely match your needs. Truebeep offers Low Band (55 MHz) and High Band (912 Mhz) systems covering the region including Maryland, the District of Columbia, and Virginia.

Frequency Band	Range in Miles	Penetration
Low Band VHF: 22-52 MHz	20	Moderate
High Band VHF: 120-222 MHz	15	Good
UHF Band: 550-800 MHz	12	Excellent

You can use any information about your industry, or your own company's special strengths relative to competitors, to accomplish the same objective as the preceding example. Make sure that the information relates to the needs of your intended, or problems that you are prepared to solve, and never directly trash your competitors. If you do it right, your beloved will assassinate the incumbent vendor/other competitors, or your competition will shoot themselves in the foot.

In reviewing other sales situations with similar prospects, you run across an analysis that you did for a client in which you evaluated the return on their investment to own the telephone lines leading to your paging terminal instead of paying ten cents per call to the local phone company. You decide to use it a few weeks later as one more way of staying in front of Frank. You also make a note to use the same tool in one of your quarterly account reviews with another client that sends a lot of pages. You send it to Frank with the following cover letter.

TRUEBEEP CORPORATION
The paging solutions company

July 28, 1999

Mr. Frank Lee Lonelee
Association of the Romantically Deprived
6200 Love Drive
Romance, Maryland 20000

Dear Frank:

In our most recent conversation we discussed whether it would be cost effective to establish tie lines from your location to our terminal. Truebeep could help you perform a feasibility study by keeping track of the aggregate message units for pagers that are active in the field. All you would need to know is what percentage of those calls originate from your local facility.

The tie line(s) would eliminate the 10 cents per call expense you currently incur, allowing you to budget a fixed mileage expense. The charges, which represent one-time start-up costs, are as follows:

- Installation charges (carrier)
- Hardware (line cards, cabinet etc. for PBX's)
- Mileage (between Maryland and Washington, DC.)

When we are ready to pursue this matter, we can easily determine the actual rates and costs necessary to initialize the Tie-Line(s), as well as ongoing charges, to determine the potential savings, as well as the payback period to recover the initial investment. One side benefit of analyzing message units on individual pagers would be the ability to determine whether the user needs to have a beeper. Low usage might indicate a misallocation of resources.

Sincerely,

Alan Salesperson
Association Paging Services Specialist

MODULE 4.1: Assignment

❑ Fill out the attached pipeline with those prospects you expect to win in the next 30 days.

30-DAY PIPELINE

Sales Representative_____
Month_____

COMPANY	PROPOSAL DATE	SALES STAGE	NEXT CONTACT	DOLLAR VOLUME

❑ Fill out the attached pipeline with those prospects you expect to win in the next 60 to 90 days.

60-90 DAY PIPELINE

Sales Representative_____
Month_____

COMPANY	PROPOSAL DATE	SALES STAGE	NEXT CONTACT	DOLLAR VOLUME

❏ Project your 30-day and 60-day sales forecast based on your pipeline.

30-DAY FORECAST

$ Pipelined	X Closing Ratio	= Forecast

60 DAY FORECAST

$ Pipelined	X Closing Ratio	= Forecast

❏ Estimate your overachievement/shortfall based on the forecast.

30-DAY PROJECTION

$ Forecasted	- Minimum Goal	= Over/Short

60 DAY PROJECTION

$ Forecasted	- Minimum Goal	= Over/Short

Disk: Assignment Folder

CHAPTER 4: A Winning Proposition

TOPIC 4.2: Proposal Development

SKILLSET TOPIC(s)
- ❏ Proposal topics
- ❏ Building a template

OBJECTIVE
Design and package your offer so that you cover any objections, eliminate any reservations, and impress the heck out of your intended.

BENEFITS
- ✓ Establish professionalism with improved packaging.
- ✓ Increase the impact with better customization.
- ✓ Help your contact sell it to his/her supervisor, if necessary.
- ✓ Add a new tool for group presentations.

> *"The proposal helps you reach the point where you can work with your prospect to iron out any areas of concern or anxiety"*

Most people do not even think about a prenuptial agreement when they consider marriage because, after all, who cares who gets the bicycle if the marriage fails? However, it is fairly common if one or both parties have significant assets, and it is generally very stressful since it could be interpreted as a lack of faith; it certainly doesn't imply the expectation of a lifelong union. In fact, the issue of having to sign a prenuptial agreement has even been known to torpedo the whole process.

Fortunately, while the sales proposal does outline the terms of the pending relationship, just like a prenuptial, and it could possibly derail the sales process if it is unprofessional or fails to address the needs and wants of the prospect, the similarity ends there.

It doesn't need to be stressful to present, and your proposal to a prospect does hold hopes of a long union. In fact, the proposal brings you and your prospect to the point where you can help them iron out any areas of concern or anxiety they may have so they can comfortably accept your offer. If you have communicated effectively, they will realize that it is a Win-Win situation for all parties and will want to do business with you.

The proposal is basically a tool that outlines the terms of the pending relationship, so you want to have enough information to impress your prospect. Unless you are dealing with the government, or you are responding to an elaborate Request for Proposal (RFP), try to be brief and concise.

Unless you need to include a ton of technical information, as would be the case with a prospect that has doubts about your technical capabilities, you can generally provide enough specific and general information in 10 to 15 pages to accomplish your objectives. You will be able to eliminate the major concerns they have expressed, as well as any perceived fears or hidden concerns they might not have shared with you but are common to all prospects (like being afraid of making a mistake).

In essence, your proposal should be designed to help the decision-maker(s) justify selecting your company to satisfy their business needs and personal hot buttons. Sounds simple, doesn't it? The truth is that except for the first few, writing a proposal should be simple.

Once you develop certain key sections that will be the same for any prospective client, there are usually only a few pages that will require thought and creativity each time you generate a new proposal. In many instances, each of the sections that you tailor for each scenario will still have a common format with only the name and numbers changing, as demonstrated in Table 4.2.1.

PROPOSAL DESIGN

COMMON SECTIONS	SECTIONS YOU CUSTOMIZE
❑ Binder/Cover	❑ Specifications
❑ Title Page	❑ Recommendations (solutions for problems/needs)
❑ Cover Letter	
❑ Table of Contents	❑ Pricing
❑ Company Overview	❑ References (should include customers in the same or similar industry, if at all possible)
❑ Product/Services	
❑ Implementation and Support	

Table 4.2.1

It is always impressive to have a professional proposal, but the packaging is especially important when there are multiple decision-makers that you may never meet. If you are not dealing directly with the final decision-maker, a proposal can help your contact get your offer approved if it is an extremely professional document he can present to his supervisor.

Bear in mind that you should propose as late as possible in your prospect's buying cycle (preferably after your competitors), and as close as possible to his projected delivery date.

Let's review the various sections of the proposal.

❑ COVER PAGE

Should include your contact's name, the date prepared, your name, etc.

❑ COVER LETTER

You could keep it simple by merely introducing the body of the proposal, as I have in the example which follows, or you can briefly outline the problems identified, and describe your proposed solutions/benefits if your proposal is going to be reviewed by someone that you will never meet.

❏ COMPANY STORY

The company story can be a powerful marketing tool because it is the first opportunity for you to help your prospect feel comfortable with choosing your company to support their needs. You could include your company's mission statement (philosophy), history, strengths, objectives, specialty, and any additional information that would indicate stability and reliability. I have found that some prospects will not read a company profile, but if it is professional-looking and has some breadth (what little you have to say in as much space as possible), it will still put their concerns about the status and capabilities of your company to rest.

❏ SPECIFICATIONS

If it is not too long, you can incorporate this section with your recommendation page. Anything that is required of you should be listed in this section. Those requirements represent part of the key to the sale in that your solutions will relate to these issues.

❏ RECOMMENDATIONS

You want to outline the solutions you are capable of providing to any problems you might have uncovered. Emphasize the solutions to their highest priority problems first, and explain the <u>benefits</u> they will experience from those solutions.

❏ PRODUCTS/SERVICES

Use as complete a description as you can, even though only a technical person would read every detail, because nontechnical people will feel reassured that there is a lot of information about your product/service and accept your company as being competent. Don't forget to include all of the things your company is capable of providing, not just the things your prospect needs at the time of the bid.

❏ PRICING

This is usually the first section reviewed by the final decision-maker(s), and is the key to winning the sale. In fact, the rest of the package is like an oyster shell, while the pricing section is the pearl inside. Always spell out what is included for their investment in microscopic detail, and list the alternative services that will be available to them in the future as their needs change. This can be very important. I have won sales where a competitor was able to offer the same auxiliary services as my company, but did not cover them.

❑ IMPLEMENTATION AND SUPPORT

I usually have a separate page for each of these topics, as you will see. At this point you want to emphasize the great lengths to which your company goes in order to insure the peace of mind of your clients. We will soon cover this section in greater detail, since it is very critical.

❑ REFERENCES

If you or your company have any other clients that are in a similar industry, include them here, and/or include high-profile accounts that have good name recognition. Always verify any references that you use. Don't laugh. Many a salesperson has used an account that they did not keep in touch with for a reference and has been extremely embarrassed (including me). If they are unhappy, regardless of the reason, work with them until they have been fully satisfied and you will have a great ally.

You will be amazed at how much your closing ratio will improve if you are creative in how you package the details of your offer, emphasizing solutions and benefits instead of features. Getting a signed agreement to deliver or implement your service will become more assumptive and less confrontational.

Before you refer to the sample of the Association proposal which follows, a brief word about the quality of your work. It defeats your purpose to develop a snappy proposal if you use sloppy copies. Always use clear, legible copies from a master copy. If you have a computer, keep the master documents on a disk so you can easily make changes for new pursuits.

It really is worth the effort to use professional presentation tools and, again, losing an account because you did <u>not</u> do your best would be a disservice to all parties. You would lose income, your employer would lose a customer, and your prospect will lose the benefits of using your product or service.

*   *   *

TOPIC 4.2: Case Study

Scenario #1

Prospect: Association of the Romantically Deprived

Much time and many affairs have passed since you first met Frank Lonelee, but you finally get the mating call and calmly agree to a meeting. When you hang up the phone, you have a silly smile from ear to ear as you see yourself enjoying the Winners Circle trip to Acapulco. You may not be able to buy your private jet yet, but at least you will get to fly on one.

You jump around like an idiot for a few minutes, hug the nearest person, and then calmly retrieve all of the information on the association to put together a proposal. After referring to your notes, you organize your solutions in a format that addresses Frank's concerns, and the concerns of the other department heads you have met, and you end up with:

PROPOSAL

TO PROVIDE

WIRELESS SERVICES

DATE: June 1, 1999

Prepared For: Mr. Frank Lee Lonelee
Association of the Romantically Deprived
6200 Love Lane
Romance, Maryland 20000

Prepared By: Alan Salesperson
Association Paging Services Specialist
Truebeep Corporation
100 Beep Boulevard
 Pageheaven, Maryland 20003

TRUEBEEP CORPORATION
The paging solutions company

June 1, 1999

Mr. Frank Lee Lonelee
Association of the Romantically Deprived
6200 Love Lane
Romance, Maryland 20000

Dear Frank:

I appreciate the time you spent helping me understand your organization's communications needs. The enclosed proposal addresses a paging services program designed specifically for your account, as per our discussions.

Truebeep's objective is the same as yours: to increase the effectiveness of your organization's external communications network. This will increase your enrollment, as well as your ability to respond to the needs of your members, which will translate to better bottom-line profitability.

You will be assigned an experienced major account manager to supervise your account using proven techniques and tools. Most importantly, follow-up will be scheduled quarterly to ensure that your account remains well managed.

I am confident that this will represent a win/win relationship for all parties and result in improved communications for your organization.

Sincerely,

Alan Salesperson
Association Paging Services Specialist
encl
AS/twp

100 Beep Boulevard, Pageheaven, Maryland 20003 (301) 999-6666

TABLE OF CONTENTS

EXECUTIVE SUMMARY

❏ Truebeep: A Pioneer in Mobile Telecommunications

Communications is at the very heart of the new technology that is reshaping American business. During the next decade, American business and industry will be riding the telecommunications revolution that is emerging from the convergence of computers and telecommunications.

Truebeep is proud to be one of the pioneers of the mobile telecommunications industry. Whether it be direct-dial paging, cellular telephone, messaging, or voice mail, Truebeep stands poised to bring growth, vitality, and added efficiency to American industry in the years ahead.

We are a pacesetter uniquely positioned to provide a wide variety of services. Truebeep has developed the most extensive network of mobile communications operations in the country, presently servicing more than 100 cities in 30 states.

From these locations, Truebeep provides a variety of telecommunications services which include various types of paging, voice message storage, automated radio, cellular telephone and other communications services designed to meet the needs of an increasingly mobile society. Also, we have invested millions in training our personnel to provide the very best in customer service.

❏ Mobile Communications for Every Need

As a leader in mobile telecommunications, we understand that no two of our customers are alike, so we offer a wide range of communications options to fit every kind of business situation. Our major concentration is on paging and related services, and we provide a number of different coverage options to serve your area, making our service more cost effective.

We also offer a variety of pricing plans, including customized billing on a quarterly, semi-annual or annual basis, plus extended term discounts. As a result, you are investing in more than just a beeper; you are getting the service and expertise of a leading telecommunications company and its subsidiaries.

Truebeep - Although pagers have been in existence for more that 20 years, recent technology has created sophisticated paging receivers that can receive more information than ever before. Truebeep is at the forefront of that technology with new services. These include the basic "numeric" pagers that display a digital message, "alphanumeric" pagers that display up to 16 messages of 230 characters each, and two-way alphanumeric pagers that can receive and respond to more complex messages with up to 6,000 characters, including e-mail.

We also offer "voice mail," which converts the voice into a digitized format that can be stored and sent by a computer. In addition, Truebeep provides a telephone answering service that allows the subscriber to connect a telephone to a central computerized message center, and with voice messaging-enhanced paging, voice messaging technology is integrated with traditional paging technology to create a new family of value-added services.

National and International Paging - Nationwide paging is now possible with our National and International Network Service. This network broadens Truebeep's capability by offering city-to-city domestic paging and international coverage in over 40 countries through the use of an orbiting communications satellite. This service is available for digital and alphanumeric paging to include voice messaging. Combined with a radio-determination satellite service from Uptight Corporation, National Network offers a unique two-way message service capable of providing routine location information for a variety of applications.

Cellular - Truebeep was one of the initial applicants for cellular licenses. A joint venture agreement with TrueSouth Corporation has enabled us to offer cellular systems in a number of cities throughout the country.

Medical Paging Services - Truebeep realizes that the medical industry is an important customer group for paging services, and our Medical Paging Service caters exclusively to this special field. We also are working to develop advanced communications systems for hospitals and medical centers.

❑ **Service and reliability you can depend on**

Truebeep is a network provider that keeps you at the leading edge of mobile communications technology. We were the first to introduce the digital pager, and we will continue to lead the industry in new products and services.

Truebeep offers a complete range of engineering, marketing, and customized services. Our own technicians serve you locally and assure that you are getting the greatest signal penetration in you area. But, most of all, our service gives you the variety of choices to make your communications more cost effective.

As a result of our excellent customer service, customized products and billing platforms, and a desire to serve, we are selected above all others for the mobile communications needs of the nation.

*   *   *

PAGING SYSTEM DESCRIPTION

Truebeep Corporation

Washington Metropolitan Area

I. ## DESCRIPTION OF TELEPHONE-TO-RADIO INTERFACE

All paging telephone trunks are input into a Gargoyle GL-3000 paging terminal. The Gargoyle terminal supports all common digital paging formats (Golay, NEC, and POCSAG) and types (Tone, Tone Voice, Numeric, and Alphanumeric). Telephone numbers on the Gargoyle can have the common tone custom greetings.

From the Gargoyle, paging data is sent via direct wires to a radio link transmitter. The radio link transmits paging information to all the paging base stations that transmit the data to the radio pagers.

II. ## DESCRIPTION OF SYSTEM FEATURES TO ENHANCE RELIABILITY

A. **TELEPHONE TRUNKS**

The paging terminal is located in Washington. All Washington numbers are served by the nearest C&P switch. This eliminates the possibility of failure due to Telephone Company Office pass-through problems. All foreign trunks, such as Annapolis and Baltimore, have alternate routing. This eliminates the possibility of exchange failure due to carrier failure.

B. **PAGING TERMINAL**

The architecture of the Gargoyle itself allows for a high degree of reliability. Unlike other terminals, which only store paging records in Random Access Memory (which is highly volatile), the Gargoyle stores all subscriber records redundantly on two independent hard disk drives. The active records are placed in Random Access Memory for efficient handling and can be automatically booted from the hard disk drives when required. Truebeep maintains spare boards for every type used in the system. This allows for independent and rapid on-site repair.

The Gargoyle paging terminal is AC powered from a "floating" non-interrupting power supply. Because the system is floating, no changes take place during a power interruption; therefore, power failures are transparent to the Gargoyle. Since the system is AC powered, the Gargoyle will automatically draw power from AC in the unlikely event of battery bank or charger failure. This configuration allows for the highest degree of power supply reliability.

C.   **RADIO LINK**

The paging terminal is directly wired to the radio link transmitter. This provides greater reliability because telephone lines are not used to reach the radio link transmitter.

The radio link transmitters are completely redundant hot-standby types. If a primary link fails, the secondary automatically takes over.

All radio link transmitters are powered by AC noninterrupting power supplies.

III.   **SYSTEM FEATURES**

A.   **HOLD TIME**

Digital pages are sent 45 to 75 seconds after completion tones are received on the phone line. Medical emergency personnel can optionally receive 5- to 15-second page times.

B.   **ALPHANUMERIC CAPABILITIES**

Truebeep offers enhanced alphanumeric features supported by the Gargoyle paging terminal. These include: message lengths up to 6,280 characters; access with computer, "dumb" terminal, or IXO; and support for all digital and alphanumeric pager models.

IV.   **SYSTEM SITE DESCRIPTIONS**

The following page lists all the paging sites in Truebeep's 900.8125 Mhz paging system. The first column shows the site's location. The second column shows the site's effective radiated power in watts The third column shows the height of the antenna above ground ground. The fourth column shows the height of the antenna above mean sea level.

*   *   *

[I hope you appreciate my not including the actual list]

SYSTEM RECOMMENDATIONS

APPLICATION

I. PERSONNEL

A) **Security staff:** Tie the tone pagers worn by security patrol into the silent alarm with a faster vibration so that they get a different silent alert on their pagers if the system is somehow breached.

B) **Maintenance:** Use a coding system to eliminate the need for voice mail.

C) **Programmers:** Use coding system (with voice mail) to eliminate the need for more expensive alphanumeric units.

D) **Management:** Can use the 25 voice mail boxes from maintenance department and upgrade 20 pagers to alphanumeric, or save an additional $600.00 per month.

II. ACCOUNT MANAGEMENT

✓ Quarterly account reviews should be scheduled to keep on top of changes in the account.

✓ Special attention needs to be given to keeping track of your pager loss rate.

✓ A summary of unusual activity should be reviewed each quarter.

* * *

ACCOUNT SPECIFICATIONS

---

1. **COVERAGE**: To include Maryland (also the Eastern Shore), Washington, DC, and Northern Virginia, as well as regional and national range. (Refer to System Description)

2. **PRODUCT MIX**: To include Sensars, Display Numeric, Tone, Tone Voice, and Alphanumeric pagers. (Refer to Pricing)

3. **FEATURES**: Dual address, voice mail storage, and VibrAlert.

3. **FAIL-SAFE MEASURES:** System redundancy. (Refer to System Description)

4. **ACCOUNT SUPPORT**: 8-hour response time. (Refer to Account Support)

*   *   *

RENTAL OPTION

MONTHLY RATE*

➢ Digital: $15.00

➢ Sensar: $25.00

➢ Alphanumeric: $20.00

➢ Alphanumeric two-way: $49.00

INCLUDES

■ Pager rental and maintenance

■ Air time (250 message units x total pagers)**

■ Dedicated Major Account Support Team

■ Quarterly account review

■ Custom billing

■ 6 spare pagers on-site

ADDITIONAL OPTIONS

➢ Group page: $ 2.75
➢ VibrAlert: $2.75
➢ Voice Mail: $4.00
➢ Regional Coverage: $8.00
➢ National Coverage: $25.00
➢ Pager Replacement Protection: $2.00
➢ 800 service use: 25 cents

* Based on 300+ pagers on a one-year agreement.

** Over-calls at 10 cents each.

LEASE OPTION

MONTHLY RATE

➢ Digital Display: $20.00

➢ Sensar: $35.00

➢ Alphanumeric: $27.50

➢ Alphanumeric two-way: $75.00

INCLUDES

- New equipment rental and maintenance
- Air time (the same as rental)
- 6 spare pagers on-site
- Custom billing
- Dedicated Major Account Support Team
- Quarterly account review

ADDITIONAL OPTIONS

➢ Group page: $2.75
➢ Vibrating feature: $2.75
➢ Voice Mail: $4.00
➢ Regional Coverage: $8.00
➢ National Coverage: $25.00
➢ Pager Replacement Protection: $2.00
➢ 800 service: 25 cents/call

SAVINGS COMPARISON

MODEL	# UNITS	CURRENT COST	PROPOSED COST	MONTHLY SAVINGS
Digital	700	$15.50	$15.00	$350.00
Tone	50	7.50	7.50	50.00
Sensar	50	25.00	25.00	(125.00)
Tone Voice	100	20.00	20.00	-0-
Alphanumeric	*100	40.00	40.00	(250.00)
Voice Mail	*150	4.00	4.00	150.00
Regional Net	85	8.00	8.00	-0-
National Net	130	25.00	25.00	390.00
VibrAlert	1,000	2.75	2.75	250.00
Group Alert	200	2.75	2.75	(50.00)
Insurance	1,000	2.00	2.00	-0-

TOTAL MONTHLY SAVINGS: $ 765.00

TOTAL ANNUAL SAVINGS: $9,180.00

PROPOSED SYSTEM CONFIGURATION

A) Eliminate 25 Voice Mail units in maintenance by using coding system

B) Swap 20 Alphanumeric for Digital with Voice Mail in programming (with coding cards)

Savings:
5 Voice Mail units @ $4.00 each =	$	20.00 per month
25 Alphanumeric @ $25 savings =	$	625.00 per month
Self insurance (see attached) =	$	875.00 per month
Total monthly savings =	$	1,520.00 per year
Total Annual Savings =	**$18,240.00**	

PAGER INSURANCE ANALYSIS

Legend
Average Pager Cost: $200.00

Insurance Costs: $2.00 per month/pager

Deductible: $50.00 per pager replacement

Monthly loss: 7.5 units

Evaluation
Insured Cost 1,000 pagers x $2.00 per month = $2,000.00 per month
+ Deductible 7.5 pagers x $50.00 deductible   =   375.00 per month
TOTAL = $2,375.00 per month

Current Losses (7.5 pagers x $200.00 ea.)   = $1,500.00 per month

Conclusion:

Self-insurance makes more sense than current insurance costs ($875.00 per month more than self-insuring). Quarterly account reviews will enable you to keep track of the lost pager rate so that insurance can be instituted when/if economical.

*   *   *

IMPLEMENTATION SUMMARY

❑ SYSTEM INITIALIZATION

Your personnel will be assigned their new pagers at a designated location. Although it is optional, we also recommend that the former vendor's pagers be swapped out at the same time to minimize any productivity loss due to schedule disruptions.

Your account manager will record user names and departments at the time of distribution (additional time for stragglers will be allocated).

A Pager Directory will then be supplied to appropriate department heads.

❑ ACCOUNT MANAGEMENT STRATEGY

✓ New pagers = fewer problems after manufacturer defect replacement for 18 to 26 months.

✓ Two spare pagers at each principle location for replacement/swap/add-on.

✓ 30-day lost pager recovery grace period (treated as a swap for 30 days).

✓ Distribution of new pagers at primary locations - notification memo to principles to schedule implementation.

✓ Voice Mail trial at no charge for 60 days.

✓ 30-day free implementation period.

✓ Departmental pager coordination the responsibility of account manager.

* * *

CONTINUED SUPPORT

A) ACCOUNT MANAGEMENT

✓ Training program will be integrated with participants' work schedule so that everyone is brought up to speed on the system, including the digital coding sequence.
✓ Old pagers will be collected at the time of distribution.
✓ You will have one point of contact for activations and service.
✓ A new pager directory will be faxed to receptionist and department heads to avoid confusion.
✓ You will have an in-house supply of spare pagers to meet forecast needs.
✓ Spare pagers will be replenished twice per month.
✓ The account activity levels will be reviewed at quarterly review meetings to analyze changes, and adjustments will be made as needed.
✓ Truebeep personnel will be on-call for weekend and evening emergencies.
✓ Runners will be available for emergency spare pager deliveries.

B) BILLING PROCEDURE

The Pager Directory created at the time of system initialization will be a comprehensive instrument containing department codes and billing numbers. The following billing statement will be issued:

❏ Each pager will be listed on the statement by pager with a single line cost.

❏ The user names will appear on the invoice with phone numbers for easy reconciliation.

❏ A summary page will group pagers by department code, with subtotals for each department.

❏ The final accounting line will list the aggregate amount due for total units in use.

*   *   *

Once you develop a basic proposal format that you can use for most situations, you will be able to take pieces of that generic proposal to use in different configurations. When you run into a special application, you just make up new materials, but keep an electronic file so that you can re-use it when you run into the same scenario again.

Also, keep a record of the customized sections of each new tool that you use in your client folder, and record the number of each form letter sent, but you don't have to keep copies of the generic documents in each client folder. You can keep copies of generic pages/sections in separate folders, or on a shelf so that you can quickly assemble a proposal for a prospect at a moment's notice.

* * *

MODULE 4.2: Exercise

❑   Which sections of a formal proposal have to be customized?

_____

_____

_____

_____

_____

_____

Appendix: Page 272
Disk: Exercise Folder

MODULE 4.2: Assignment

Develop a proposal for your own prospect-in-progress based on your notes from the Strategy section.

<u>CUSTOMIZED PROPOSAL SECTIONS:</u>

1) Cover letter

2) Account specifications

3) Recommendations

4) Offer

5) Savings analysis

6) Account management and support

CHAPTER 4: A Winning Proposition

TOPIC 4.3: Your Sales Presentation

SKILLSET TOPIC(s)
❑ **Presenting the proposal**
❑ **Group presentation tools**

OBJECTIVE
To make sure that your presentation covers solutions and benefits, and to work out any compromises necessary to help your contact get approval to move to the next step, like closing, testing, etc.

BENEFITS
✓ Establishes professionalism.
✓ Ensures that all of your solutions and benefits are effectively presented.
✓ Eliminates unspoken concerns.
✓ Sets up a Win-Win situation for all parties.
✓ Helps the influencer and/or recommender get approval when you are unable to get to the final decision-maker.
✓ Reduces anxiety (yours) and provides peace of mind (theirs).

> "If you really want to boost your success rate, NEVER drop off the proposal unless there is no possible way that you can present it personally."

When you propose to a prospect, you are asking them to trust you to deliver what you promise, and you are implying that you will love and cherish the account for as long as they remain a client.

You are also committing to help them resolve any problems that might crop up, and offering to keep them abreast of new technology as it develops.

The proposal that you use to outline those promises and impress your intended with the solutions that you have developed is a valuable tool. However, <u>how</u> you propose is just as important. If you really want to boost your success rate, the first rule that I would suggest you follow is to NEVER drop off the proposal at the front desk or pop it in the mail if there is any way that you can present it personally.

When you are presenting the proposal in person, you can read body language while you try to resolve any objections that come up. You lose the opportunity to do that or respond to questions if you drop off the proposal. Unless all of your competitors are in the same boat, that would place you at a disadvantage.

THE PROPOSITION

When you do your presentation, begin by referring to some part of your most recent conversation as a bridge between the previous meeting and the current one. After the foreplay, you might want to suggest that instead of reading every page during this meeting, it might make more sense to briefly summarize each section and let them read in greater detail at their convenience.

At that point you can hand them a copy(s) of your formal proposal, summarize the key points of the previous meeting, and explain how those issues led you to the solutions that you have outlined and your company's offer.

You then walk them through the highlights of your company story, discuss your customer service commitment briefly, and have the client open the proposal at the page where you describe the problems and solutions, followed by the pricing page.

At the end of your presentation you want to ask if you have missed anything and address any questions that may come up at this point. If you know they are not ready to sign an agreement, for instance if they have to get approval from corporate, you should close for the next step, like a follow-up phone call or testing coverage, if you have not already done so.

On the other hand, if you think they are ready to make a decision, at the conclusion of the presentation you could finalize the sale as follows:

Summary: *"Clearly, you will have our corporate commitment of superior support for your company, as do our other major accounts. As a result, you will only have to spend 2% to 5% of your time managing your communications network. Any service that you had to commit more time to than that could become relatively expensive, wouldn't you agree?"*

Wait 30 seconds. If they beg you to let them sign up, do it now! If they don't offer to sign up at this point, you need to offer them the opportunity to do so. I often get an agreement signed by integrating that act into an action plan rollout. You start helping them plan out the transition, keeping them involved, as follows:

Transition: *"The next step, to make sure that the implementation strategy, operation, and support go as smooth as glass, is to set aside a few moments to develop our strategy for setting up the account. That will give us an opportunity to determine what actions we have to take and when, in order to ensure that we are on target for a perfect landing. Would this time on this date be convenient, or would this alternative date be better for you?"* Once the meeting is scheduled, you also need to ask them who else they feel might need to be there.

If others do need to be included, you should offer to write a memo inviting them to the meeting. Whether you or your contact issues the memo, make sure that it includes a list of any information that they would need to bring. Explain in the memo that the purpose of the meeting is to develop an implementation strategy to avoid downtime and errors. You would end that topic by saying, *"After all, without adequate support, the greatest implementation in the world will still leave you with a lot of work afterwards. I am looking forward to our next meeting on ------."*

Close: If they agree to the next appointment, and there are no unresolved negotiation issues, take out an agreement and put it in front of yourself and say: *"I will need your approval so that I can submit the order as soon as possible. That way I can make sure that my support staff has enough time to order the equipment, program and test them, set up a user directory, and design your billing format."*

Smile, put your pen on the agreement, move it so that it faces them, and shut up. Rather than looking at them, which might make them (and you) feel pressured, you could begin transferring information from your note pad to their client file.

After they have signed, explain the agreement and any attachments, and put your initials next to any amendments. Make sure that you leave them a copy of the agreement, and you should also add a copy to their Support Guide, which we will cover later.

If they don't sign up after your presentation, listen to their reason(s). If you recognize it as an objection, try to overcome it as you normally would. If you are facing an objection that you were not aware of, you still want to close, but instead of asking for a signature you are asking them to agree to the next step, whatever that may be.

This is probably a good time for me to briefly define the difference between a condition and an objection as we use the terms in this text (we will get into detail later).

As you know, an objection is usually a blocking device, indicating that the prospect has doubts or unanswered questions. You can often eliminate the objection by using the standard technique of restating what they said to make sure that you understood them, verifying that it is the only problem, resolving the issue, and asking for the order again.

An example of an objection would be when someone is not convinced that your company will be able to deliver on their commitments. You can usually overcome that concern by demonstrating the capabilities of your company, and by giving them the name of other satisfied clients.

Conditions, on the other hand, are circumstances that delay a sale, like budget considerations, an acquisition, a change in management, and/or a contractual obligation. They prevent the sale from being consummated until that condition expires or is circumvented. Normally, you would know about any conditions from your research efforts, and would resolve them before you do the closing presentation.

When you present the agreement, if a prospect says that they can't sign the agreement, and their reason is a real condition that you were not aware of, agree that what they are saying makes sense. You could even sheepishly admit that you sometimes get a little bit too excited at the opportunity to help a company get the most out of their investment. You will have another chance to get a signed agreement at the implementation meeting.

By the way, if you feel uncomfortable presenting an agreement as part of the closing process, I would like you to consider something. When you are trying to win an account, you have to believe that they should choose you, and that the benefit will be mutual. If your product/service can solve a problem, increase efficiency, and/or save money, etc., it is in their best interests buy from you. In a sense, you would be doing them an injustice if you don't make the sale.

Needless to say, even if you lose the bid, you still want to send your contact a letter thanking them for giving you the opportunity to work with them. You might also want to keep in touch at three- to six-month intervals, depending on how long their new contract is, so that you can rebid the account when their contract comes up for renewal.

Aside from the issue of contract expiration, anything could happen over a year or two. For one thing, your competitor might drop the ball, thereby leaving the account vulnerable. Another possibility is that their needs might change over time, and/or the needs of their customers, at which point you might end up having an edge over the competitor who originally won the bid.

We will return to closing right after I address something that happens fairly often when you are dealing with large companies. Since they usually have multiple parties involved in the purchase process, you will sometimes find yourself presenting to a group. When that happens, you might find the next topic helpful.

GROUP ACTIVITIES

Years ago I was one of several managers who were invited to lecture at a training seminar for the account executives of the company that we worked for. My topic was the presentation, so I grabbed a copy of the best proposal I could find and made some notes about how to present it effectively.

Imagine my surprise when I arrived at the conference center, looked at the schedule, and found that I was supposed to cover presenting the features, advantages, and benefits of our product, not the proposal itself. Even worse, someone else was already scheduled to talk about the proposal. I nearly swallowed the whole bagel I was nibbling on. I briefly considered asking the other manager to trade, but sanity prevailed and I ate four pastries instead.

It just so happened that I had recently done a presentation to a group of eight directors with one of my major account executives. I still had the materials in my briefcase, so I decided to talk about how to present to a large group. Although it wasn't exactly the topic I was originally scheduled to present, it went over well, and I only gained a little weight from the pastries.

The presentation tools that I covered in that seminar are really effective for group presentations, and they also represent a terrific way to distinguish yourself from your competitors, so I want to share them with you. As you know, most salespeople hand copies of the proposal to an individual or a group, and then tediously go through it page by page. Let me suggest a different approach.

The next time you present to a group, tell them that you plan to hit the key pages, like recommendations and the pricing, and then give a brief summary of the rest of the proposal. Suggest that they can read the full proposal at their leisure, so that they can give it a thorough review. Since a large group will probably not approve the sale on the spot anyway, you are not really risking anything, but you will accomplish several important objectives.

Presenting the summary will allow you to control the group, instead of having them leafing through the proposal while you are trying to explain the solutions and benefits to them. It also helps you organize your information in a concise format that will have more immediate impact than the proposal, which is usually very detailed. Finally, you will be able to get your point across to anyone who is not as good at understanding concepts as images.

As for the summary itself, you basically create three slides or overheads with the following titles: Initial Evaluation, Account Transition, and System (or program) Management. In each section you list the issues that are a priority to the company/group from your critical information notes, the solutions to those issues, and the benefits to the organization. As you will see, you want to include every imaginable service/capability that you can provide. You should also duplicate any solution or service that affects more than one section, which will make your list even more impressive.

By outlining every conceivable solution that you can offer, and leveraging any advantage/capability that you can think of, you will be able to address all of the possible concerns of the various individuals who will be involved in the buying cycle. After all, other than the major issues and solutions, you never know exactly what will hit a particular individual's hot buttons.

Once you have handed out copies of your proposal and answered any preliminary questions your audience might have, you lead into the presentation by presenting your first slide (Figure 4.3.1) in the following manner:

Introduction: *"I have taken the liberty of organizing the issues that you have expressed concerns about into three basic areas so that I can briefly summarize the solutions and benefits that we can provide. Please feel free to ask questions at any time. The first area relates to your initial evaluation of our capabilities."*

PRELIMINARY EVALUATION

ISSUES	CAPABILITIES	BENEFITS
Performance	A. COVERAGE ✓ Local, regional, and national paging B. PENETRATION ✓ Confirmed by our trial pager use C. SYSTEM MANAGEMENT ✓ Real-time alarm reporting ✓ 24-Hour/7-day-a-week technical staff ✓ Simulcast and Link technology ✓ Proactive site management	Improved communications Improved customer response Fewer field trips
Support	• Delivery service • Maintenance directory • Dedicated account manager	Management time savings
Risk	❑ 89-year successful track record ❑ Thousands of satisfied customers ❑ Emergency response team	Low

Figure 4.3.1

Needless to say, you want to customize this section as much as possible. As an example, if you represent a large company, stress how many thousands of happy customers you have, especially high-profile accounts the audience would recognize, and any in their industry. If you represent a small company that does not have high-profile accounts, emphasize the personalized attention and the super-responsive customer support they will get.

If you know of any legitimate concerns that are not yet resolved, like testing, billing issues, or software development that has not yet been completed, assure them that they have every right to be concerned about those issues before you cover the solutions. That will typically disarm their defenses so that they can listen with an open mind.

As you walk them through the different points under Capabilities, embellish each one with a brief description as to how it will provide a solution to their problem or concerns. Do the same thing with the Benefits section, including hard numbers and ROI numbers for things like cost savings and/or increased efficiency.

When you are done, answer any questions, and then try the following trial close:

"As you can see, we are fully qualified to meet your current and future needs, wouldn't you agree?"

If you get a positive response you can move on. If you don't get an enthusiastic reaction, you need to stop and ask if you have missed anything before you move on, and restate whatever points are necessary to get a smile on their faces.

While the section that we just covered is pretty standard, in the sense that you already have lots to say about the capabilities of your company, the second and third sections are more flexible, giving you an opportunity to be creative.

In the second section you are covering the account delivery or setup. People are afraid of change, so even if there has been no stated concern, you want to focus on anything that you can do as a company, and as an individual, to make the process easy for them and virtually foolproof, as demonstrated in Figure 4.3.2. I cover some tools and strategies in the last two chapters that will be helpful for this section of your presentation.

Introduction: *"We all want the implementation to be painless, with no loss of productivity, so now let's review the support that you can expect during the transition."*

ACCOUNT TRANSITION

ISSUES	CAPABILITIES	BENEFITS
Preparation	✓ Assess coverage, and improve signal strength in weak transmission areas ✓ Co-develop implementation plan at prestrategy meeting ✓ Coordinate transition schedule ✓ Complete and distribute a User Directory ✓ Create new billing format	Eliminate missed communication Improve internal communication Eliminate billing inconvenience
Delivery	➤ Painless transition to new service coordinated by on-site technician and customer service representative	Eliminate lost productivity and confusion
Support	❑ On-site technician ❑ Dedicated customer service team ❑ Experience with large customers	Reduce internal management time Immediate problem resolution

Figure 4.3.2

Try to think of every positive thing that you can say about how you will ensure a trouble-free delivery, but avoid technical jargon that is only used in your industry. At the same time, buzz words like "strategic account management," and phrases like "consulting with the client to develop solutions," are good.

When you have finished elaborating on the solutions that are a high priority, and have briefly mentioned all of the additional services that will help solve any unexpected problems that might crop up, you want to test the waters with another trial close, like:

"Would you agree that the implementation strategy we have developed together makes good sense?"

If you don't get enthusiastic agreement at this point, ...

The last phase of your presentation is easily the most important. At this point you are providing your prospects the peace of mind of knowing that selecting your company will not blow up in their faces, as demonstrated in Figure 4.3.3.

For example, let's assume that you know that the Association of the Romantically Deprived is in the process of acquiring new companies, and might be merging with their largest competitor, which would make them a huge potential account. In order to tap into that issue, you might want to use the following type of approach:

Introduction: *" Our long-term, and final concern would have to be the ongoing account support that will free you up to do your job, and how we can ensure that it continues to do so for the foreseeable future. I also want to discuss how we will be able to provide efficient solutions to unanticipated problems.*

Scheduled account reviews will provide you with "peace of mind" in the sense that we monitor future potential product/service savings and potential problems, so that you can concentrate on more important issues and challenges.

Let me take a moment to outline exactly how we provide that support, because it is easily as important as how well our system works, wouldn't you agree?

SYSTEM MANAGEMENT

ISSUES	CAPABILITIES	BENEFITS
Short-term	✓ On-site technician	Rapid problem resolution
Mid-term	✓ Scheduled follow-up visits by dedicated customer service representative ✓ Billing flexibility ✓ Usage reports	Smooth operation
Long-term	✓ Quarterly reviews ✓ New products assessment and recommendation ✓ National Account Program available in the event that you need to outsource total system management	Proactive problem control Automatic system enhancements

Figure 4.3.3

"The ongoing support is in many ways the most critical aspect of our service for many of our clients. For instance, having scheduled account reviews enables us to head off any potential problems early instead of waiting until contract renewal. Wouldn't it be nice to have the peace of mind <u>to be able to</u> dedicate your time to other issues that should rightfully take precedence without worrying about your paging service?"

Once you have reviewed this section, you follow the same steps we discussed earlier. Unless there are any obvious things you need take care of first, close for an appointment to finalize the details. Needless to say, if they are actually ready to buy, get the order signed.

In case you were wondering, I use a PowerPoint presentation that I can easily change for each situation, but you can use several other formats, such as overheads or slides. You could even add it to a presentation book, but it is better to customize it for each prospect.

* * *

MODULE 4.3: Assignment

1) State your company's capabilities and the benefits of your product/service on the forms that follow.

2) Highlight the hot buttons for your prospect-in-progress (use different colors if you are working with more than one contact).

PRELIMINARY EVALUATION

ISSUES	CAPABILITIES	BENEFITS
Performance		
Support		Management time savings
Risk		Low

ACCOUNT TRANSITION

ISSUES	CAPABILITIES	BENEFITS
Preparation		
Delivery		Eliminate lost productivity and confusion
Support		Reduce internal management time Immediate problem resolution

SYSTEM MANAGEMENT

ISSUES	CAPABILITIES	BENEFITS
Short-term		
Mid-term		Smooth operation
Long-term		Proactive problem control Automatic system enhancements

Disk: Assignment Folder

CHAPTER 4: A Winning Proposition

TOPIC 4.4: Closing the Sale

SKILLSET TOPIC(s)
- ❑ Closing issues
- ❑ Negotiating
- ❑ Building Value
- ❑ Top-down selling

OBJECTIVE

To help the prospect make the right decision by resolving any defined and hidden objections, and position yourself to negotiate terms (but only if necessary).

BENEFITS

- ✓ Distinguish between conditions and objections to ensure that you use the right closing techniques.
- ✓ Increase your average sale revenue.
- ✓ Authenticate the value of your product/service.
- ✓ Improve your negotiation skills.
- ✓ Leave your client in a Win-Win situation.

> *"Distinguishing the difference between a condition and an objection is critical. It affects how you react to each situation, which will ultimately determine the probability of your winning or losing the account."*

When a prospect is not the final decision-maker, and they tell you that they need to review other bids, it usually means that they have to present an analysis of several proposals to their supervisor for approval.

That is a condition, not an objection, so the last thing you want to do is try to push them to make a decision on the spot. It is no different than a romantic situation: if you make your mate angry, you might find yourself sleeping on the couch with only the cat for company.

If your relationship with your contact is strong enough, your best bet is to bracket the bid by getting them to look at other vendors that you know are more expensive, or you could try to shut out your most effective competitors by having your prospect set criteria that only you can satisfy. If you are unable to use that approach, present as professional a proposal as possible for them to forward to their boss (make two or more copies, as needed).

However, if you are dealing with the owner, the issue of getting bids could be treated like an objection. If you have a technical advantage that nobody else offers, like special coverage the prospect needs, the issue shouldn't even come up. But, as we discussed earlier, many companies have a policy of getting multiple bids.

When a final decision-maker, and especially the owner, tells you he is going to get more bids, try the following close.

THE "GETTING BIDS" RESPONSE

"Mr. Prospect, I have no problem with your getting bids, because I know that we are relatively competitive with any vendor that has a COMPARABLE product/service. However, some of my clients have admitted that sometimes even when they saved a little by shopping, the time they spent on shopping ended up being more expensive than the small savings that resulted. I was just wondering if you have ever had that experience?"

Using this approach could lead you right back to an opportunity to justifying the order, based upon whatever competitive edge you might have.

Let's briefly revisit the issue of conditions versus objections, because distinguishing between the two affects how you react to the specific sales situations you encounter, and your response affects your probability of winning the account.

As you know, you have to listen to an objection, repeat it to make sure you understand it, isolate it (make sure that it is the only thing preventing the decision-maker from making a decision), resolve it, and then ask them to approve the agreement again.

While this technique will work on objections, it can sometimes be counterproductive if a legitimate condition exists. If your contact <u>cannot</u> make the decision because of circumstances that are not within their control, even the best closing techniques will fail. In fact, at some point every salesperson has lost an account they should have won by trying to push their contact when he was unable to move.

Again, my definition of a condition is a circumstance preventing the sale that is outside of the control of you and the decision-maker until that condition is resolved. One of the most common and obvious conditions that you will encounter is a contractual obligation. That is sort of like someone being married (which can spoil a perfectly good affair).

For example, if your prospect has a year left on their contract with their current vendor, you both have an insurmountable short-term problem. There are a few exceptions, like when the vendor has failed to fulfill the terms of their contract and is therefore in Breach of Contract. That could represent grounds to terminate the contract without penalty, but it is a rare occurrence, and very few companies want to pursue that remedy in court.

A less obvious but still very common condition is the internal approval process that most decision-makers in large companies have to comply with, like having to get three bids. Unless your product or service is of a critical nature, most decision-makers will not override their internal approval process to speed up the acquisition. If you were in their shoes, would you? Even if some salesperson showed you how to save two percent on your budget, which might be thousands of dollars per year, would you jeopardize your job to move as fast as that salesperson would <u>like</u> you to?

Again, you have to be patient, persuasive, and professional while you work with your contact to achieve a satisfactory resolution to any conditions that exist. There is no need to put unreasonable pressure on your contact, nor should you give up hope prematurely.

However, even after you have resolved any conditions that may be present, many people will give you an objection before they agree to buy. After all, people are conditioned to say no. Their parents said "No" to them a million times before they reached adulthood. As a result, you will still have to use your closing skills, but when you use some of the professional sales tools and techniques that we are covering, you will eliminate a lot of those objections before you even ask for the order. They will be more likely to trust you, and less hesitant about making the decision when you demonstrate that you are a professional.

While I have no intention of rehashing the same old "Sales 101" closing techniques that you already know, I would like to suggest a pretty good way to overcome an objection that is rarely voiced by most prospects.

When someone asks you for customer references, it usually relates to their perception of your company's ability to deliver and support their account, because at some point everyone has experienced a problem with something they bought that was never totally resolved. There is nothing more frustrating than being jerked around by a company, whereas if the problem was handled promptly and courteously, people usually become customers for life.

When your prospect asks for references, ask them if customer service and support after delivery is important to them. If they agree that the service after the sale is just as important as the initial product/service performance and quality issues, you can pre-close with the following statement:

The "References" Response

"If I tried to persuade you that we had the greatest service in the world, you would probably remember that the other two salespeople you met this morning said the same thing. However, when I include some customer references who will attest to the quality of our support when a rare problem did occur, you might believe that we actually have the best quality support available at any cost. Isn't that what you really want?"

If there is no reason for them not to buy from you at that time, get the prospect to call your references on the spot. Once you have set up the right conditions, you simply close by pulling out the agreement ...

Believe me, your competition will rarely get the drop on you if you use this approach. The concept will be even more credible to the prospect if you have already gone to great lengths in trying to sell them by using professional tools and a well-thought-out strategy.

Let's move on to cover a subject I think you will find quite interesting.

PAINTING A ROSY PICTURE

What if you are involved in a sales situation with a prospect that does not have to take the lowest bid, yet they insist on a better price? You can assume that you are facing an objection, and worse, that it is the always-revolting "Price" objection.

You and I both know that somebody, somewhere, will always be able to offer a similar product/service for less money than you can, regardless of which company you work for. Whether your prospect is going to receive the same value for their investment from the competing company is debatable.

The first thing that you want to do is prove that they will not receive the same value for their investment from your competitor by justifying exactly how your product or service will represent a better value for them, but without bashing the competitor(s). That is the crux of the section that we are about to review.

Even if your product or service will not save them <u>more</u> than the competitor could, the way that you present your case might be better, and it is the <u>perceived</u> value that counts, anyway.

For example, if you and a competitor offer the same product/service at basically the same price, but you show your contact how they will save money, and your competitor fails to, you would probably win that sale without major grief and discounting required.

Taking the time to figure out the value of your product/service to your prospective client, and a method of describing that benefit in measurable terms will impress your contact to no end. This is called calculating the ROI, or Return on Investment, but I prefer *"Pencil Selling,"* because you can use this technique on the spot to close a sale.

Of course, you do want to call it an ROI calculation when you present it to the prospect. It is my experience that when you explain the following types of calculations to your client, you will have them thinking about options OTHER THAN whether or not to buy from you. Sometimes this strategy will even psych them out of automatically trying to get a discount.

Calculating the Return on Investment impact takes a little bit of practice, but at least it gives you an opportunity to use some of the math skills you learned in school that you thought were a total waste of time.

The basic concept is demonstrated in Example 4.4.1. You can use the basic formula as a template for new selling situations by substituting the specific variables of your sales scenario in the appropriate sections.

ROI CALCULATION

EXAMPLE A

If using your product/service can save a company 8 hours per employee/month, and they have 50 employees, it would represent the following savings:

Legend

```
Employee hourly pay           = $20.00
internal cost (22% x $20.00)  = $ 4.40
(for taxes, benefits, & holidays)
TOTAL HOURLY COST             = $24.40
```

Once you have established the base numbers that are involved, you simply calculate the value of the potential savings for your prospect as follows:

Contract Value Calculation:

```
50 employees x $24.40 savings per hour  =  $   1,220 per hour
X 8 hours savings per employee/month    =  $   9,760 per month
3-year contract = $ 9,760 mo x 36 months =  $351,360 total savings
```

OR YOU COULD USE THE FOLLOWING CALCULATIONS:

Legend

```
Hourly employee productivity  =    $200.00
Gross profit margin           =    12%
```

Productivity Gain Calculation

```
8 hour savings per employee/mo X $200.00 =  $    1,600.00
$1,600.00 incr productivity X 50 employees =  $   80,000.00
$80,000.00 x 36-month contract           =  $2,880,000.00
$2,880,000.00 incr productivity X 12% GPM =  $  345,000.00 savings
```

Example 4.4.1

EXAMPLE B

Now let's assume that your product or service was going to cost that company more money than they would save in the short term, but more than justify the investment over time. We will compare two different types of scenarios. In the first it will cost them less than they save, and in the second, a little more (we will use the $9,760.00 per month savings figure).

Scenario 1

Monthly payment required   = $ 8,760.00
Projected monthly savings   = $ 9,760.00
Net monthly gain to company = $ 1,000.00

- Total gain over term of contract = $36,000.00
- This could also be stated in terms of a break-even point for the company, as follows:
- Total investment ($8,760.00 X 36 months) = $314,360.00
- Break-even point ($9,760.00 savings into $314,360.00) = 32.3 months

Scenario 2

Monthly payment required = $10,000.00
Projected monthly savings = $ 9,760.00

Total cost over term of contract = $12,240.00

NOTE: Obviously, Situation A would be easier to sell, but Situation B could also be sold if the return in savings would continue after the payments stopped, as would be the case if you were installing a system or piece of equipment. In that scenario they would be able to recover their $12,240.00 within a couple of months after they stop making payments, which is basically a 34-month break-even point.

Example 4.4.1 (Continued)

You can easily make up a standard form that you can bring to the meeting and fill it out in front of the prospect with his help (have him supply the base numbers), or you can work out the numbers on a blank sheet of paper. Either way, it will impress him and potentially give him a neat tool to present to the next person in line if he is not the final decision-maker.

Any time that you use more than one way of calculating the return on someone's investment, you would naturally present to him the best-looking results.

You can also use the same technique to demonstrate your expertise by helping him analyze things such as whether he should buy or lease, as demonstrated in Example 4.4.2. You will again be distracting him from the primary thing that would otherwise be on their mind: talking you out of some of your commission.

PAGER INSURANCE ANALYSIS

LEGEND
Pager Cost: $150.00
Insurance Costs: $2.00 per month/pager
Deductible: $50.00 per pager replacement

Scenario A:
A 125-pager account historically loses 15 pagers per year and self-insures

Calculation:

Current Costs (15 pagers x $150.00 per replacement) = $2,250 per year
versus:
Insured Cost 125 pagers x $24.00 per year   = $3,000 per year
 + Deductible 15 pagers x $50.00 deductible = $ 750 per year
                                    TOTAL =$3,750 per year

Recommendation:
Insurance would cost $1,500 more than self insuring, so you should continue to self-insure, and the quarterly account review will enable us to keep track of your lost pager rate so that insurance can be instituted when/if economical.

Scenario B:
A 125-pager account historically loses 30 pagers per year and self-insures

Calculation:

Current Costs (30 pagers x $150 replacement) = $4,500 per year
                                    versus
Insured Cost 125 pagers x $24.00 per year   = $3,000 per year
    + deductible 30 pager x $50 replacement = $1,500 per year
TOTAL = $4,500 per year

Recommendation:
At this point insurance might make sense, but if you choose to continue to self-insure, then you absolutely have to help keep track of the lost pagers on a quarterly basis to catch any increase in lost pagers, which would make insurance a more cost-effective option at that time.

Example 4.4.2

No matter how good you are at pencil selling, some people will insist on negotiating the price, in which case you might consider the advice that follows to be somewhat helpful.

THE ART OF COMPROMISE

Most sales involve negotiation, whether it occurs well before you propose or afterwards, and it does not always relate to the price. The negotiations might revolve around things like the terms of payment, which peripheral services are included, the cost and availability of upgrades, and the support of that account.

Negotiating is not an area in which I claim to be an expert, so I recommend additional reading on your part. At this point I merely hope to stimulate your interest in learning more about negotiating skills, since it is a vital part of large account sales. The more you know about it, the more confident you will feel; and the more you practice, the better you will become.

To me, negotiating has always been partly instinctive, since my objective is invariably to place all parties concerned in a win-win situation.

When it comes to price negotiations, my personal favorite is "The Strip." For this strategy to be an option, you have to go into a selling situation with a fair price, but include as many bells and whistles as possible. This is also sometimes referred to as "Top-Down Selling," since you start with the "Top of the Line" package but are prepared to shed features/services as needed to reach a price that your client is willing to accept.

That way, you may be able to drop your pants without giving up any commission at all, and it is less embarrassing to drop your price when you can justify the reduction. (The same thing holds true with your pants.) Obviously, if your service is exactly the same as your competitor's, you may still have to negotiate on the price when you are <u>markedly</u> more expensive.

A time-tested formula that has worked with a great deal of success for me in that type of situation is:

The "Split the Difference" Response

"Mr./Ms. prospect, we seem to be pretty far apart in terms of price, but you agree that you would benefit from our product/service. Perhaps there is a reasonable price point that falls somewhere between our two positions that we would both find acceptable. I wouldn't be doing you justice without trying to negotiate with my manager to get you that price."

You save face by implying that you are looking out for the best interests of your prospect if any discounting is required, and it is also the perfect lead-in for you to ask for referrals.

If the prospect can make a decision immediately, you can call your manager and explain that you need a super favor. Describe the situation and ask for the best possible price if she signs up today. If the sale will take longer because of some condition(s), then you can just come back with a new price for her to compare against other bids or factor into their budget. Once you have gotten her a better deal, asking for referrals is rarely seen as an imposition.

Be careful when you use this strategy. You want to associate pricing with THEM (your company), and not imply that you have any authority to affect pricing issues. If you imply that you can discount the list price, you will be amazed how fast you can become the bad guy who is being unreasonable instead of your boss (who is paid to be the bad guy).

You are essentially trying to have three winners emerge from any business negotiation: the company you represent, the client that you hope to sell, and yourself.

Finally, I always try to leave something on the table <u>after</u> the sale is closed, so that my client feels that he/she was a good negotiator. It might only be an extra manual, or a small gift with our company logo on it. The gesture will cost my company very little, but it ends up making my clients feel like winners (which we all are).

*   *   *

TOPIC 4.4: Case Study

Scenario #1

Prospect: Association of the Romantically Deprived

Sometimes your original offer is not exactly snapped up. Even worse, the few prospects who do get excited almost always have no direct budget authority to do anything about it, while those who have the authority to sign the check normally deliberate decisions at great length before reacting. That might be why they are authorized. The Association proves to be no exception to the rule, so you decide to use a couple of new tricks to heat up a lukewarm situation.

The first one demonstrates the pricing breaks that the Association is getting compared to other (smaller) accounts. It can potentially help you avoid a future price objection.

The second tool can help you create new pricing breaks without having to give up part of your commission, as you would when forced to offer unwarranted discounting.

TRUEBEEP CORPORATION
The paging solutions company

July 21, 1999

Mr. Frank Lee Lonelee
Association of the Romantically Deprived
6200 Love Drive
Romance, Maryland 20000

Dear Frank:

As per your request, I have calculated the rate reduction/savings to the Association of the Romantically Deprived for pricing concessions on Truebeep's paging services. A summary is attached for your review.

With the help of Ms. Bee Frustrated, we have developed a paging program tailored to the requirements of your organization, rather than merely replacing hardware.

Our negotiations have been based on a Win-Win perspective. Should Truebeep be selected to support your paging needs, we will gain an excellent reference, as well as a reasonable stream of revenue. Your paging system will be on a 900 Mhz UHF system with excellent coverage and penetration due to our vast array of multiple transmission facilities.

We understand that it is your responsibility to select a vendor who will provide you with the latest technology, quality products, and the best service at a competitive cost. Your vendor should also help you control cost, simplify billing procedures, and develop proactive strategies to enhance system performance on an ongoing basis. This, in fact, describes Truebeep's commitment to our customers.

Sincerely,

Alan Salesperson
Association Paging Services Specialist

Enclosure
AS/twp

cc: Ms. Bee Frustrated

100 Beep Boulevard . Pageheaven . Maryland . 20003 . (301) 999-6666

SAVINGS SUMMARY

MODEL	LIST	YOUR PRICE	UNIT SAVINGS	# OF UNITS	MONTHLY SAVINGS
DISPLAY	20.00	15.00	5.00	750	3750.00
BEEPS	10.00	7.50	2.50	50	125.00
CUTE	35.00	25.00	10.00	50	500.00
SPARE UNITS (10)	250.00	-0-	25.00	10	250.00
DOES IT ALL	50.00	40.00	10.00	50	500.00
SPEAKS BACK	25.00	20.00	5.00	100	500.00
NATIONAL NET	30.00	25.00	5.00	80	400.00
VIBRALERT	3.00	2.75	.25	1,000	250.00
GROUP CALL	3.00	2.75	.25	200	50.00
INSURANCE	2.50	2.00	.50	1,000	500.00
			TOTAL	**SAVINGS**	**$6,825.00**

ONE-TIME FEES WAIVED

Connect Fee	$2.75 x 1,000 Units	$2,750.00
Regional Coverage	$5.00 x 85 Units	$ 425.00
Voice Mail	$4.00 x 150 Units (30 day trial)	$ 600.00

Total Fees Waived **$3,775.00**

TOTAL FIRST YEAR SAVINGS $85,675.00

Since there are a lot of divisions of the Association of the Romantically Deprived, you get permission to offer them a significant pricing break if you can sign up some new divisions.

The following Blanket Pricing Agreement could just as easily be used to justify discounting for a prospect when your price is not quite competitive enough to win their business.

You can get your supervisor to agree by doing your homework, and by putting some numbers representing the business potential of other divisions in a market survey as we discussed earlier. This would help to get your supervisor excited, and they can use it to get their supervisor...

The way that you word the proposal can even serve to give your contact some recognition as a good negotiator. In your cover letter to your contact, use a phrase like "As per your request, I have received approval to reduce our fees." or "The enclosed document is the formal agreement to the terms that you negotiated."

TRUEBEEP CORPORATION
The paging solutions company

July 28, 1999

GROUP RATE SCHEDULE

At the option of the Association of the Romantically Deprived, Truebeep hereby agrees to extend volume-sensitive pricing for paging equipment and services to all related departments, locations, and divisions as per the terms and conditions negotiated by Mr. Frank Lee Lonelee.

Truebeep would bear the expense of notifying the various entities not included in the original scope of the agreement. Credit towards unit volume discounts would be cumulative to all parties, audit to be performed at Truebeep's expense.

VOLUME	DIGITAL	ALPHANUMERIC
1,001-1,500	$7.25	$14.50
1,501-2,000	$7.00	$14.00

Signature
  Billy I. Doosit, General Manager
  Truebeep
  100 Beep Boulevard
  Pageheaven, Maryland 20003

1000 Beep Boulevard . Pageheaven . Maryland . 20003 . (301) 999-6666

MODULE 4.4: Exercise

❏   Calculate the ROI for NetCom.

CRITICAL INFORMATION: Based on the responses from your investigation, you know that your service will be more expensive than SlowBeep is currently charging, so you have to concentrate on efficiency savings/cost reduction. Using your two-way pagers can save NetCom 30 minutes per employee/day, and they have 400 service technicians in the field. Their labor cost is $40.00 per hour, and they bill $150.00 per hour.

A) LABOR COST SAVINGS

Labor Cost

Savings Calculation (Annual):

B) INCREASED BILLING POTENTIAL

Calculation (Annual):

MODULE 4.4: Assignment

❑ Calculate the ROI for your own prospect-in-progress.

CRITICAL INFORMATION:

A) COST REDUCTION (if your product/service is less expensive)

Calculation (Annual):

```
┌──────────────────────────────────────────────────┐
│                                                    │
│                                                    │
│                                                    │
│                                                    │
│                                                    │
└──────────────────────────────────────────────────┘
```

B) LABOR COST SAVINGS

Labor Cost

```
┌─────────────────────────────────┐
│                                  │
│                                  │
│                                  │
│                                  │
└─────────────────────────────────┘
```

Savings Calculation (Annual):

```
┌─────────────────────────────────────────────┐
│                                             │
│                                             │
│                                             │
│                                             │
│                                             │
│                                             │
└─────────────────────────────────────────────┘
```

C) INCREASED BILLING POTENTIAL

Calculation (Annual):

```
┌─────────────────────────────────────────────┐
│                                             │
│                                             │
│                                             │
│                                             │
│                                             │
└─────────────────────────────────────────────┘
```

CHAPTER FIVE

Delivery Dilemmas

"When the adrenaline rush of winning the account is just a distant memory, and problems seem to crop up at every turn, you might sometimes find yourself wishing that your client had said no. Fortunately, that is only a temporary state of affairs...unless you blow it."

CHAPTER 5: Delivery Dilemmas

TOPIC 5.1: Implementing the Account

SKILLSET TOPIC(s)
- ❑ **Avoiding delivery disasters**
- ❑ **Keeping the blush on the relationship**
- ❑ **Setting the foundation for more business**

OBJECTIVE

To help you avoid delivery disasters and keep the blush on the relationship by identifying which parties are most affected by the delivery and implementation, coordinating the event, and creating effective account management tools.

BENEFITS

- ✓ Avoid problems by conducting implementation strategy meeting(s) prior to the delivery.
- ✓ Prevent disillusionment by following through with <u>EVERY</u> commitment.
- ✓ Prevent customer disillusionment by being equally attentive after delivery.
- ✓ Increase customer loyalty.
- ✓ Use the new account as a platform for more business.
- ✓ Get references and referrals.

> "If you want to turn a delivery snafu into a positive, keep your client informed about your progress in resolving the problem on a timely basis, even when the news is bad."

As long as nothing goes wrong, the delivery is usually anticlimactic (unlike a honeymoon). That is probably a good thing, because if you are like me, the chase will have totally worn you out way before.

It can also be the most fun part of the sales process. To begin with, if things go smoothly you are a hero, and it is really great to have someone who loves you (besides your mother). You probably also enjoy those moments when your client thanks you for your great support, which they will do often if you use the tools we are going to cover.

Last, but not least, it can represent a really terrific opportunity for you to get more business from the same department and/or other affiliated user groups, and who doesn't like that?

However, while most deliveries go as smooth as silk, occasionally they don't go quite as well as you planned, and, as you know, that can be quite stressful. But having problems during delivery doesn't necessarily mean that you have lost the opportunity to position yourself for future business, as long as you are willing to do more than simply fix the problem.

The first thing that you want to do is to take their call and express your sympathy. Even if you are unable to do anything about it at that moment, you will at least give your client the opportunity to vent their frustration. After they have vented, make sure that you get specific details as to what went wrong, and guide them through it if they are unfamiliar with your product/service or the way your company operates. Sometimes it is just a simple misunderstanding that can easily be cleared up.

If it turns out to be a genuine snafu, but it is clear that a phone call to one of your departments will correct the error, tell your client what you are going to do, and then take care of it immediately. If you delay, you give your client more time to stew about it, and, even worse, if you get really busy you might forget. This is all pretty standard procedure, and it should get you off of the hook.

However, if you want to turn the situation into a positive, call your client right back to tell them how long it should take to be resolved (be conservative), and then ask them to let you know if the problem is not corrected by the time that it should be. I personally make one last call to verify that the problem is resolved, even if they don't call me, because, occasionally, when a problem goes on too long the customer gets disgusted and calls my competitor instead of me.

If the problem that your client describes turns out to be something unique, you should review other accounts that you have worked on to see if there is a potential solution that has worked in a similar situation. If that fails, try talking to your manager and/or associates. One of them might know of a solution, or at least be able to help you brainstorm. Whatever the results, make sure that you call your client back within a reasonable period of time to update them, even if the news is bad. That way they will know that you are trying to resolve the problem, which should make them a lot more tolerant.

Once the problem has been fixed, be sure to send your contact a "welcome aboard" letter or card within a week. You should also consider stopping by around a month after the implementation with donuts or a gift with your company logo on it, something inexpensive. Needless to say, you should use the same strategy with new customers who did not have any problems.

It is also a good idea at the time of delivery to reconfirm exactly who you will be dealing with to manage the account on an ongoing basis. Sometimes it is not the person who originally ordered your product/service, and at other times there may be multiple parties you were not aware of in the support chain (not counting additional contacts that you need to make, such as the accounts payable manager, etc.).

Even if there are multiple parties involved in the direct chain, try to get one point of contact designated for all problem calls so that you don't have to train a lot of people or explain yourself over and over again. You can usually sell the idea by explaining that one point of contact makes it easier to track activity and ensure that all new orders are authorized.

If you have to manage multiple contacts in an account, make sure that you train them well. Unfortunately, their mistakes can sometimes be just as disruptive as if your company dropped the ball. Setting up one point of contact is especially important if you have to deal with multiple users directly. Instead of having dozens of people calling you with problems, it is a whole lot easier to have them call one person at your client company, who then calls you. Again, if you can't avoid it, make sure that you train them well.

In order to avoid abuse and billing problems, find out who is authorized to order more product/service, and notify your billing department while you are setting up the account, if not before. Make sure that you ask about other departments, branches, or subsidiaries that you might want to talk to, perhaps to offer high volume price breaks.

If your company offers it, you should also suggest an employee discount program while you are implementing the account. As long as things go smoothly, you should have a warm reception.

From that point on you will have the perfect reason to stop by between any scheduled account reviews to update their Support Guide, at which point you will be able to introduce new products or services and get even more referrals.

Finally, make a point to keep track of your contact in the company. If he leaves, you need to find out who replaced him as soon as possible to avoid the account becoming a cluster because the replacement is clueless. You might also be able to follow your old contact to the new company he accepts a position with, and sell him all over again. Since you have already been involved in a torrid affair with him at the prior company, it should be a lot easier to sell to him the second time around.

* * *

TOPIC 5.1: Case Study

Scenario #1

Prospect: Association of the Romantically Deprived

Speaking of the honeymoon, Frank finally signs an agreement. Of course, by now you are too old to enjoy the trip you have won, but you send him a "welcome aboard" letter anyway, because you are a nice guy.

TRUEBEEP CORPORATION
The paging solutions company

September 8, 1999

Mr. Frank Lee Lonelee
Association of the Romantically Deprived
6200 Love Drive
Romance, Maryland 20000

Dear Frank:

I wanted to thank you for selecting Truebeep to support your paging needs. We are looking forward to a mutually rewarding relationship in the future.

This is to confirm that our implementation will be scheduled for Tuesday, September 20 and Thursday September 22 from 1:00 p.m. until close of business. I will be on site to distribute your pagers. Additional time will be allocated as needed.

Please contact me at (301) 555-9999 should you find it necessary to adjust this schedule.

Sincerely,

Alan Salesperson
Association Paging Services Specialist

100 Beep Boulevard . Pageheaven . Maryland . 20003 . (301) 999-6666

It turns out to be a good thing that you did send the "welcome aboard" letter to Frank and your other new paging clients. Soon after the delivery, a fire breaks out in the building where your terminal is located, so all of your clients are unable to use their pagers for three days.

Once everything has been put back on track, you get everyone who was affected credits against their accounts to make up for the interrupted service, and you send them letters to let them know how much the credits will be for. This preemptive move has them eating out of your hand. (Not that they would have paid anyway, but at least they feel like they didn't have to mug you to get the credit.)

Regardless of the cause, if your clients have been deprived of the use of your product/service, or suffered any major inconvenience, it might pay for you to request credits for their accounts. If you are successful, your clients will love you (or at least forgive you). Even if you don't get the credit approved, you will at least feel good about trying. What do you have to lose? Either way, your clients will be grateful because you "went to bat for them," and you might even get a referral or two for your trouble.

TRUEBEEP CORPORATION
The paging solutions company

November 28, 1999

Mr. Frank Lee Lonelee
Association of the Romantically Deprived
6200 Love Drive
Romance, Maryland 20000

Dear Frank:

I wanted to apologize for the recent unavoidable interruption of your paging services, which as you know, resulted from a fire at our transmission facilities. Enclosed, please find a summary of the credit to your account which has been approved in view of the loss of service, although it in no way makes up for the inconvenience that you have suffered.

I very much appreciate your patience in this matter, and look forward to meeting with you for our quarterly review in November.

Sincerely,

Alan Salesperson
Association Paging Services Specialist

Enclosure

ACCOUNT CREDIT SUMMARY

Assigned Department	Account #	Monthly Fees	Credit Applied
Service	987609	$1,000.00	$100.00
Maintenance	986545	etc.	etc.
Security	985621		
Management	989081		
Installation	984325		
Programmers	983661		
		Total credit	$750.00

You feel great about getting the credit, but you decide to also do something else to make Frank happy. In looking through your files, you find a coding system that you designed for a property management company that you can use for the Association, which owns some apartment complexes.

The codes would let the maintenance people know which building was affected, and what type of problem occurred. You call Frank, get the number of one of their apartment managers, and find out that people are paged for three types of situations.

The first type of situation, and the most critical, occurs when they have to respond to an emergency like an apartment catching fire or flooding. Since this type of situation can either be life-threatening and/or cause serious property damage, it requires an immediate response.

The second type of situation that occurs is less critical, but requires a response within a reasonably short period of time. For instance, the property manager might want someone along for emotional support at an eviction. Unless the tenant has a baseball bat, you could complete the section of wallpaper you were working on before responding.

The third type of situation, like a personal message, typically merits a very low priority. The person being paged would only need to check in before leaving work, since the message might be to bring milk home.

You quickly put together a coding reference sheet, which you send to the apartment managers (with a copy for Frank).

SITUATION RESPONSE CODES

PRIORITY	PROBLEM/ISSUE	APARTMENT #
1	**1.** Fire **2.** Flood **3.** Sewer backup **4.** Girlfriend's husband called	
2	**1.** Lock-out **2.** Skip-out **3.** Vendor **4.** Rich aunt called	
3	**1.** Work order **2.** Personal message **3.** Poor aunt called	

A message received by one of their apartment managers might look like this:

1 - 2 – 141

This would mean that there was some form of flooding in building #141 that needed their immediate attention before the carpeting, floorboards, or perhaps even the apartment below becomes affected. The manager could go directly to the building in question with the appropriate tools, instead of being forced to go to the maintenance building first. Saving the manager that one step could be a lifesaver in the event of a fire.

There might be similar creative tools that you can develop to leverage your position with an existing account, depending on how they utilize your product/service. Add whatever tools you develop to your file to use for future prospects, and add it to your client's Account Support Guide (next topic).

*   *   *

CHAPTER 5: Delivery Dilemmas

TOPIC 5.2: Account Management Tools

SKILLSET TOPIC(s)
- ❑ Organizing an account profile
- ❑ Developing an Account Management Guide
- ❑ Additional account management tools

OBJECTIVE
To develop and implement account management tools that will enable you to prevent problems and maximize account growth.

BENEFITS
- ✓ Confirm your professionalism.
- ✓ Reassure the decision-maker(s).
- ✓ Diminish your contact's workload.
- ✓ Proactively eliminate potential problems.
- ✓ Maximize account growth with scheduled account reviews.
- ✓ Eliminate internal and external confusion.
- ✓ Maintain control of account.

> *"The tendency to relax after delivery can sometimes lead to careless mistakes. After all the work already invested, it makes no sense at all to become sloppy and run the risk of losing the account."*

Most of us tend to get a little excited when we are about to deliver a really large order, and we certainly get frustrated if there is a problem getting the product/service delivered or set up in time, etc.

However, once you have delivered the account there is a natural tendency to relax, which can sometimes lead to careless mistakes, sort of like taking your spouse for granted. Both situations can lead to a divorce, and after all the work that you have already invested, it makes no sense at all to become sloppy and run the risk of losing the account (or your spouse).

Even worse, besides losing that client, you will also lose any potential referrals to other divisions or large accounts through contacts they might know.

You can avoid that problem if you develop a directory your new client can keep in their office and refer to for information about your product/service. I call it an Account Support Guide, and it is basically an account profile that contains key information about the account in a format that both you and the client can use to keep track of the activity in the account.

Developing the profile is fairly simple. You start with copies of any correspondence that you have already sent, and the proposal that you developed for your prospect, which you organize into separate sections in a binder. You then add new sections for things like the minutes (notes) from meetings that you attend, a user directory, notes about special billing issues, and specific account requirements, as demonstrated in Figure 5.2.1. Don't sweat it; there are examples in the case study.

Developing the Support Guide for your customers and prospects will require very little work on your part because most of the content is done when you write your proposal. Besides, the benefit to you and the customer will more than justify the effort. It will enable you to provide proactive account management services to your clients, eliminating problems before they happen instead of having to spend all of your time fixing problems after they occur.

No competitor will offer this level of account support, so you will rarely lose one of your clients to a competitor.

Make sure that you also keep your own account file to which you can add internal paperwork from your company such as approval forms, memos authorizing pricing concessions, and copies of internal correspondence.

ACCOUNT SUPPORT GUIDE

INITIAL CONTENTS

- Proposal
- Agreement
- Memo(s) (generated to their departments)
- User Directory (if needed)
- Account management and billing arrangement
- Quarterly Account Review schedule (outlining those areas that need to be monitored)

ASSEMBLY

Pull the following documents from your client profile/folder and put them into in a three-ring binder.

1) All correspondence

2) Parts from their proposal
 - Executive Summary
 - Recommendations
 - Capabilities
 - Pricing

3) Copy of their agreement

FUTURE ADDITIONS

- Exception Reports
- Quarterly Review Agendas
- Quarterly Review Minutes
- Optional products/services available (add as introduced)

Figure 5.2.1

Once you have completed the delivery, you simply add any new documents that you use during the relationship, like correspondence, quarterly review summaries, new product updates, bulletins, etc. There are some really great examples of different types of tools that you can use demonstrated in the case study.

Some companies already have collateral material that you can use for the guide, like numbered tabs and binders with the company logo imprinted, while others may not. Once upon a time, when we couldn't get the company to pay, my sales team ordered customized color inserts with the company logo and special tabs, and the whole team shared the cost. After our regional manager saw how well it worked, he got approval to reimburse the salespeople and pay for all future supplies.

If your company does not have materials for the binder, you might want to consider a small personal investment. The materials might cost around $5.00, which would be tax deductible, so the cost would be a pittance compared to the commissions that you will earn. If you use the guide as part of your closing strategy, and you close 40% of the prospects that you propose to, you might invest $12.50 per account sold.

That is not a lot of money when you think about the value of your time. On average, you probably spend a minimum of 20 hours working on a major prospect, and sometimes as much as 50 hours. That includes finding, qualifying, the blind date, developing the proposal, presenting the solutions, going back to your manager for new pricing, etc.

If your income is around $60,000 per year, your time is worth $30.00 per hour. So, if it takes an average of 25 hours to win a major sale, you are investing at least $750.00 in time to win one account. In other words, if you are in the $60k income range this type of out-of-pocket investment is peanuts, and if you aren't, these tools can help you get there.

Anyway, it just makes good sense for you to spend a few dollars on your prospect. That is really no different than spending a few dollars to take someone special on a great date. Well, there are a couple of differences: your investment for materials is tax deductible, while your dates are not. The other major difference is that while you might get a kiss from your date, which is nice, the major accounts that you win could help you win a trip to some exotic island populated only by members of the opposite sex. (You can dream.)

As I mentioned earlier, you can even use this tool to help close the sale. If you do not get approval when you present the proposal, you want to schedule another meeting rather than waiting for a phone call.

What better reason for a meeting than to review the Account Support Guide and the implementation/ delivery strategy to ensure that everything goes smoothly?

If they do not agree to another meeting, you are probably not going to get the sale. That might be a good time to restate the benefits of your program.

If they do agree to meet again, after you have discussed the steps of the delivery and reviewed the Account Support Guide, you try to close again as follows:

"Let's make sure the behind-the-scenes people have enough time to ensure that you get maximum support and a smooth transition, by placing the order now."

*   *   *

TOPIC 5.2: Case Study

Scenario #1

Prospect: Association of the Romantically Deprived

At this point you are ready to give Frank Lonelee his Account Support Guide. The cover page contains the account name, address, telephone number, and contact name that your internal support staff can use. As a result, anyone who takes over the account when you are promoted or reassigned will have no problem keeping everything running smoothly.

It really helps both organizations to have a record of the principals involved. For example, sometimes the client contact name will change when your original contact realizes that they would rather not be directly responsible for the mechanics of the account. More often it will be your internal account support staff that will change, and you will want to make sure that your client is notified.

The second section of that page is equally important, since it identifies the correct party for your client to call should any problems develop. Any problem that might occur would be best handled by whoever is directly responsible for that particular aspect of the account. Should your client contact the wrong party, there is a high probability that the problem would not be resolved in a timely fashion.

The last section is self-explanatory, and even I do not have the nerve to bore your further. Obviously, you need to update this document as contact personnel change, and it can provide you with an excellent reason for contacting your client to keep your name uppermost in their minds when they make future purchase decisions, or when other people ask them to refer an alternative vendor.

ACCOUNT SUPPORT CONTACTS

Account Name   _____

Contact   _____

Telephone #   _____

SUPPORT TEAM

Account Executive   _____

Office Telephone #   _____

Pager Telephone #   _____

Car Telephone #   _____

Customer Service   _____

Office Telephone #   _____

LOCAL TRUEBEEP LOCATIONS

FASTCALL   WILLCALL
999 Call Road   999 Ring Road
xxx, Md. 99999   xxx, Md. 88888
(301) 555-9999   (301) 555-8888

SECTION 1

❑ Account Management Overview

The first section of the Account Support Guide represents an outline of how you intend to manage the account. This information becomes critical when you prepare to deliver, at which point your relationship consists of two parts: setting up the account, and supporting the account after it has been debugged.

While the following example demonstrates the support of a paging account, the basic concept would be similar for many products and services. You want to summarize how you will set up the account to minimize the associated workload of your contact or whoever will be responsible for managing your product or service. At the same time, you are also explaining what you plan to do to ensure a smooth transition and provide ongoing proactive account support.

This accomplishes two very important objectives: it clearly indicates that a coherent plan will be in place to help your contact supervise future product/service utilization to ensure optimum efficiency, and it reinforces the impression that you have successfully done the same thing for other major users.

This will contribute significantly to the peace of mind of your intended, and help ensure that you get a boost in your paycheck.

ACCOUNT MANAGEMENT STRATEGY

❏ **SYSTEM IMPLEMENTATION**

- Members of your staff will be assigned their new pagers at the location you designate. Although it is optional, we also recommend that the former vendor's pagers be swapped out at the same time to minimize any productivity loss due to schedule disruptions.

- Your account manager will record user names and departments at the time of distribution (additional time for stragglers will be allocated).

- A Pager Directory will then be supplied to appropriate department heads.

❏ **ONGOING SUPPORT**

➤ Truebeep personnel will be on call for weekend emergency service.

➤ Your account manager will make a premise call on a scheduled basis to make sure there are no problems.

➤ A dedicated customer service representative will be your one point of contact when your account manager is working with another client.

➤ Runners will be available for deliveries of outbound pagers and for emergency swaps, etc.

SECTION 2

❑ Billing Overview

When you are setting up a new account, bear in mind that each organization has billing software limitations, a unique internal billing and accounts payable process, and various cost tracking needs.

As a salesperson, you should try to accomplish two related objectives when addressing billing issues with potential clients. First, make sure that you fully understand the capabilities and limitations of your own organization, and always restrict your commitment to clients so that any promised services fall within parameters that your company can deliver.

Your second objective is to learn enough about the needs of your prospective client to be able to present them with a billing system that meets their needs. If you can improve on their current system, promote it and the resulting benefits. If not, at least emphasize the fact that they will not lose any of the benefits that they currently enjoy.

Of course, you never want to misrepresent the capabilities of your organization, since that will inevitably come back to haunt you.

If you need to do something special for a prospect, sometimes your operations or administrative manager will be able to design a custom billing package for a large user, and this new program can be offered to other customers and prospects. Sell your operations manager on the benefits that other accounts might gain, with very little additional work beyond that first application (just like your using previous sales tools, with a minor adjustment, for your new prospects).

Once you have enough information to set up the account, add it to their file to be initiated when you are able to schedule implementation. This would include memos to the appropriate individuals affected to announce schedule dates, etc. You might add something like the following example to your client's Support Guide.

BILLING PROCEDURES

The Pager Directory that is created at the time of system initialization will be a comprehensive instrument containing department codes and billing numbers. The following billing statement will be issued:

➢ Each pager will be listed on the statement by user and phone number, with single line cost summary.

➢ A summary page will group pagers by department code, with subtotals for each department.

➢ The final line on the summary page will list the aggregate amount due for the total units in use.

➢ In the event of a billing dispute, a billing review teleconference may be scheduled at the convenience of the client, and an account audit performed as necessary.

➢ Electronic billing is also available.

SECTION 3

❏ User Directory

Some products/services do not require a directory of users, inventory codes assigned to facilitate inventory control for your client, or any related documentation.

In paging, you might need to use a programming summary for group numbers, or some other tool that can help your client and internal staff keep track of some aspect of their product/service consumption or distribution patterns (how they use it).

When you sell a telephone system to a new client, for example, each extension would need to be programmed for the assigned user, giving each his or her speed-dial numbers, telephone numbers (trunks) that need to appear or be accessible from their instrument, and what model they get. Including specialized information in the Account Support Guide that you need to develop for internal purposes will require very little extra work. On the other hand, once you have a record of the specific details relating to the needs of individual users, you can easily avoid any possible misunderstandings.

This will also ensure that your own support staff has the necessary details to enable them to set up the account correctly, to prevent problems from occurring in the first place. The exact format is not as important as the content. You need to make sure that the key fields of information are included to enable your contact to keep track of every aspect of the account, as well as enable your internal account support staff to control the account. You could use a format to record specific user information that looks like the example that follows.

USER DIRECTORY				
MODEL TYPE	SERIAL #	USER	BEEPER #	DEPARTMENT

SECTION 4

❏ Account Management Reports

When you show up for a scheduled account review meeting, one of the greatest tools that you can utilize to confirm or improve your credibility is a simple document that reviews the activity that occurred during the period preceding your meeting. Not the normal expected activity, but any activity that was <u>not</u> anticipated.

This exception summary may also provide you with the necessary information to make recommendations to change some aspect of the account to improve your client's position.

Using the paging example, you might be able to recommend self-insuring if the new pager loss pattern justifies dropping insurance coverage, or suggest that they bill by different cost centers if there is an appreciable discrepancy in consumption patterns.

This report would join all of the others in the account support section of the Account Support Guide. An example of an exception report might appear as follows:

EXCEPTION REPORT			
DATE	PROBLEM	ACTION	STATUS
11/1/99	Broken alpha pager	Swapped for new	New Serial # xxxx
11/14/99	Hired two sales reps	Added 2 alpha	New serial # xxxx
			New serial # xxxx
11/29/99	Etc.		

I make up new account management or activity tracking tools for my clients as necessary to manage the account effectively, and add them to a general file for future use. The sample documents that complete Frank's Account Support Guide could be amended for virtually any customer's account and activity management

---

ISSUES TO MONITOR

PAGER LOSS PATTERN

➢ Currently lose 7.5 pagers per month
➢ Have recommended self-insuring
➢ Need to flag the account if they reach 10 lost pagers lost per month, since at 11.5 units they would need to seriously begin thinking about taking insurance

MARKETING

➢ Sales staff could use customized voice mail ID, which is supposed to be available within 3 months (we'll see)

BILLING

➢ Make sure that billing shows departmental consumption (except for managers, who pay the bills)

The Issues to Monitor list is changed after every account review meeting to reflect the new issues that have to be monitored until the next meeting, and perhaps remind you to introduce a new product or service to them. It is also the foundation of the next scheduled review meeting, as follows:

QUARTERLY REVIEW AGENDA

DATE: First week of the quarter

LOCATION: 6200 Love Lane

ISSUES TO ADDRESS

- ✓ Exception report

- ✓ Pager loss rate

- ✓ Spare pager inventory

- ✓ Projected needs

- ✓ New technology (particularly if it satisfies a current need)

The next scheduled account review would then revolve around the issues that you targeted at the preceding meeting, which you have described in your Issues to Monitor section.

Finally, you make notes from each meeting to add to the Account Support Guide, as follows:

MINUTES: Quarterly Review

DATE: Second week of quarter

LOCATION: 6200 Love Lane

ISSUES ADDRESSED

✓ **Exception report:** Two pagers had over 1,000 messages; need to investigate

✓ **Pager loss rate:** The same as preceding period

✓ **Spare inventory:** Need one extra spare

✓ **Projected needs:** Expanding marketing department within next couple of months, need to check back next month and order at least six new consecutive phone numbers

ISSUES TO BE ADDRESSED

➢ Same, (will change date on old one, but that will be our secret)

NOTES

Candy has gained some weight (that is no secret, and I won't include that in the official minutes that I put into her Account Support Guide)

As you can see, the preceding documents are easy to develop and modify. They will help you and your contact keep track of their account, and provide you with a reason to make sales calls between scheduled reviews.

Also, since it sits on your client's shelf, it will constantly remind them of what a wonderful lover you are, so they will be much less likely to succumb to the advances of future suitors.

*   *   *

TOPIC 5.2: Exercise

1) What are the account management areas that you need to address?

_____

_____

_____

_____

2) Describe the sections of your client's Account Support Guide

Initial:

_____

_____

_____

_____

_____

_____

_____

Future:

_____

_____

_____

_____

Appendix: Page 274
Disk: Exercise Folder

TOPIC 5.2: Assignment

1) Collect all related documentation for your hot pursuit.

2) Outline an implementation program.

3) Develop an account review and management tools.

    a. Issues to monitor
    b. Quarterly Review Agenda
    c. Account Review Minutes
    d. Any other forms that you think will look good to your contact

CHAPTER SIX

Keeping the Flame Alive

"After years of working together, it is quite natural to become comfortable with your clients, even to the point of sometimes taking the relationship for granted. However, that is definitely not an effective way to ensure that you and your client will grow old together."

CHAPTER 6: Keeping the Flame Alive

TOPIC 6.1: Consultative Account Management

SKILLSET TOPIC(s)
- ☐ **Avoiding common pitfalls**
- ☐ **Effective account management tools**
- ☐ **Customer care strategies**

OBJECTIVE

To help you develop an effective proactive account management system to prevent problems and sell more products and services within the account.

BENEFITS
- ✓. Avoid catastrophes that can result in the loss of a large client by maintaining an active profile.
- ✓ Eliminate confusion with a proactive account management plan.
- ✓ Increase new sales activity within your accounts with consultative tools.
- ✓ Get more referrals into other major companies.

> "If your customer activity is mostly unproductive, like visiting too often with customers that have no growth potential, you might be unconsciously setting yourself up for failure."

Many families today consist of dual working spouses, in which case raising a family takes careful planning. The decision to have children can represent a major sacrifice of income to the household, and the wife may face a potential career conflict.

Fortunately, in sales you can grow your family without any of those disadvantages. The bigger your family of clients, the better your income and career growth, and the greater the perks, like awards, trips, etc. Best of all, the offspring in your family put money into your checking account instead of taking it out.

Growing your business can be very lucrative, but before we review a proven strategy for cultivating that growth, I need to cover a critical issue. You probably already know that managing major accounts can open the door to a very real problem: it is all too easy to fall into the trap of spending too much of your time calling on established accounts instead of also finding new business. Needless to say, it is much easier going to a friendly climate than facing potential rejection.

What you may not be aware of are the early warning signs of account addiction. If you know what to look for, you can usually head off the problem before it becomes critical. The symptoms of account addiction would include:

ADDICTIVE SYMPTOMS

- ➢ Stopping off at customers with no objective.
- ➢ Stopping off at customers after losing a bid or being shot down by two or three targeted prospects.
- ➢ No new customers signed up for an unreasonably long period, and no new prospects in the pipeline.
- ➢ No new prospecting calls around your client base.
- ➢ Too much time spent with accounts that have no possible growth potential.
- ➢ Meeting with nondecision-makers too frequently, again with no agenda.

If you occasionally find yourself doing one or two of those things, don't worry about it. If you frequently find yourself guilty of three or more, you may be unconsciously setting yourself up for failure. You might be thinking; "What am I supposed to do?" The best strategy that I know of is to work in some cold calls around your customer calls. If you are in the area anyway, it only takes about 15 minutes or less to talk to the receptionist at the businesses on either side and across the street.

You should also be making a lot more customer calls on accounts that have the potential to grow than on those that do not. While there is no perfect formula, you could try using an adjusted schedule that is similar to the Customer TLC Program in Table 6.1.1.

CUSTOMER TLC PROGRAM

ACCOUNT	VISITS	STRATEGY
Small/no growth	9 months	✓ Call every 6 months
Small/growth	6 months	✓ Call 3 months ✓ card 6 months
Medium/no growth	4 months	✓ Call 2 months ✓ letter 6 month ✓ holiday card
Medium/growth	2 months	✓ Call monthly ✓ lunch 3 months ✓ holiday card
Large/no growth	2 months	✓ Call monthly ✓ lunch 3 months ✓ holiday card
Large/growth	Monthly	✓ Call 2 weeks ✓ lunch monthly ✓ holiday card
Referral source	Monthly	✓ Send flowers ✓ lunch 3 months ✓ holiday card

Table 6.1.1

Your account visits should always be scheduled and have a clear objective, such as to review the account, introduce new products, and/or make new contacts within the account. Naturally, the visit to a very large client with multiple departments or multiple locations will take longer than with a smaller client, so you may want to plan your day around that scheduled visit.

You should never go out of your way to make an unscheduled customer call if it means that you will basically be out of operation the whole day, unless you have an objective that will directly contribute to your immediate productivity.

With the small company, you should be there to ask for referrals or to get a letter of recommendation; with the larger account you would want to get introduced to another department/ location head or be able to introduce new products.

One last caution: while large accounts can be very lucrative, try to resist the temptation of relying on a few big accounts for all of your productivity. It is all too often the case that a salesperson will be too busy supporting their customers to find new business, only to find themselves suddenly hanging around with all the free time in the world (and very little income) when they lose one or two large clients. If you do not add new accounts to your base, and you lose one or two large ones, you might find yourself in a major dry spell until your new pipelined accounts are romanced through their buying cycle.

While you want to be careful, you also want to work smart, and growing your account base is definitely easier than winning a new account from scratch. You have to work your fingers to the bone to win a new prospect, and you have only a 30% - 40% probability of winning their account, whereas you have better than an 80% probability of selling any prospect that you are referred to. Even better, you have a 90% probability of selling more products or services to your existing customers as their needs increase (if they are happy with you).

One of the ways that you can get an immediate boost in sales from this workshop would be to develop an Account Support Guide for some of your current major clients instead of waiting until you approach new prospects. Think of how much your clients will enjoy having a reference manual containing every transactional document pertaining to their account at their fingertips.

It can also be very profitable for you. Think about how great it would be if, during a brief review of their account, you were able to show your client that their account needs have changed, and a new service or product that you offer will now be able to save them even more money than before.

They would surely be ecstatic, and you would probably also be fairly pleased if you could sell them more of your product/service. Bear in mind that when you can show a client how a minor change in his existing product/service will save him money, you create enormous goodwill since that makes him look good to his boss.

Sometimes you might find yourself in a position where the right recommendation might not be in your own best interests in the short-term. Make the recommendation(s) anyway, even if they do not involve short-term gains for you. Doing the right thing will make you feel good, and will lead to much greater gains in the long-term when you introduce new products and get referrals.

Take the example of pager protection that we reviewed in Pencil Selling. You recommended that your client self-insure their pagers, which might mean less commission for you, but it was the right thing to do for your client.

If you treat your clients fairly, your credibility would be unquestioned, so that when you do have new products to introduce your client will trust you and buy more from you without your having to pressure them. They will also sing your praises to everyone they talk to, which will result in even more sales. You would probably never lose that account, even when things do go wrong.

Other than providing strong support, the most effective way to penetrate deeper into an established account is to help them lower their rates. As we discussed in the previous section, you can often accomplish that objective with large organizations as a result of sales to related departments, divisions, or locations. Most large companies will qualify for some type of volume pricing discount if you can group some of their independent user groups together.

Of course, the new groups that are added (departments, etc.) will also benefit from the reduction in cost, and you will be able to offer more competitive pricing than other competitors without having lost any commission. If your company does not currently offer volume-sensitive pricing, you can use the market survey strategy to motivate them to change their mind.

There is no easy way to be successful in sales, and account base penetration requires hard work, just like new client development. Penetrating and expanding an existing account requires research, technical writing, telephone and correspondence follow-up, good record keeping, and just plain old-fashioned persistence.

I personally enjoy cultivating an existing account far more than finding a new one, and don't mind the hard work a bit. Isn't it a bit foolish not to work extra hard for your clients, when you think of all the time that it takes to find and win one? Why would you want to do it all over again unless you have no choice? For you to find and win a new major account, even using targeted marketing, you would probably have to go through the following steps:

About 75 telephone attempts to get 60 contact names, which leads to 60 letters, leading to 150 telephone attempts, which results in 45 telephone contacts, which leads to 15 blind dates, which might generate 12 proposals, which would probably net you 7 clients (short-term).

And, finally, it makes good sense to keep romancing your major clients because they tend to grow pretty fast. If you think about it, smaller accounts that you win may have the same percentage of growth as a large account, but will not generate nearly as much new business for you. When a company that is 20 times the size of another has a 5% growth spurt, the smaller company would have to grow 100% to equal their net gain. While few companies expand 100% in a year, many large accounts have annual growth of 5% or a lot more.

Now let's look into the distant future, when you have become a superstar, and, of course, you start taking for granted the wonderful clients who made you what you are.

*   *   *

CHAPTER 6: Keeping the Flame Alive

TOPIC 6.2: Customer Retention

SKILLSET TOPIC(s)
❑ **Proactive account management**

OBJECTIVE
To review a technique that will enable you to maintain a good relationship with the appropriate decision-makers that control your account so that you can grow the business, get referrals, and stop competitors from stealing them.

BENEFITS
✓ Eliminate potential dissatisfaction buildup.
✓ Get your accounts to add more products and services.
✓ Outmaneuver your competitors.
✓ Minimize new prospecting requirements.

> *"Taking care of problems that crop up is good, but it will not protect you from competitors if they are creative in their approach, and can offer a better price when soliciting your clients."*

Have you ever wondered how some relationships last for decades when so many others don't? In my experience, they were reinforced and rejuvenated with little thoughtful gestures along the way.

It may have been something as simple as giving sentimental cards or flowers for no special reason, and it very likely included having long, intimate conversations. When you compare this to keeping a customer, the concept is very similar.

While taking care of any problems that crop up is certainly the basis for customer retention, all that will do is keep them from calling another company to shop because they are ticked off at you, or your company. Unfortunately, it will not necessarily protect you from the competitors who solicit your clients if they are creative in their approach and can offer a better price.

If you want your customers to grow old with you, I want you to consider going a little beyond the normal call of duty. For instance, if someone handles a problem for one of your customers, instead of assuming that everything is under control unless you get an irate phone call, get in the habit of calling your contact afterwards to make sure that the problem has been resolved.

Happy customers will give you more business and refer others. If you add a few simple steps to your routine, you can even get your customers to avoid your competitor's calls. Instead of just taking care of problems, show your affection by doing little things to keep them happy, like calling occasionally just to say hi, and sending clippings of articles that they might be interested in.

You should also let them know about any new ideas that you learn from other accounts like theirs, and notify them about any advances in technology that might affect their accounts, even if it will not result in a sale.

Other touches that can really satisfy your relationship and keep the romance alive would include things like sending a letter of congratulations when your contact is promoted, or when her son graduates from college. Of course, a periodic stop-by with donuts is always appreciated, as is an invitation to lunch, etc.

Actually, it just makes good sense to work a little harder for someone who has already bought from you than for a complete stranger. A happy customer will be more likely to buy additional services from you in the future, and she could be a strong reference for you, which is especially helpful when you are dealing with a prospect who is nervous about making a commitment to use your product or service.

A call to one of your happy customers would certainly help to eliminate any of the possible reservations that might exist in the mind of your prospect. If you do a good job for your customers, some of them will be happy to write you a letter stating their satisfaction. Their letters of recommendation will go a long way in helping you establish credibility with new prospects who are really just looking for proven solutions and reliable support.

Unfortunately, those nice touches will go up in flames if your customer has a major problem that goes unresolved for an unreasonable period of time. So you still have to make sure that he is happy with his service, and that can sometimes get a bit complicated.

How many arguments have you had with your significant other that were really not about the issues you were arguing about? Your relationships with your customers are no different, including the fact that they don't always tell you when something is bothering them. You may only find out that there was a problem when they give their business to another vendor. That typically happens because people want to avoid confrontation, such as telling you that your company has dropped the ball.

One way to eliminate that potential problem is to call periodically to find out if there are any problems that may not yet have been reported, in addition to keeping on top of your accounts to make sure that any problems you know about have been resolved. This should also be one of your objectives at regularly-scheduled account reviews (refer to TLC Program, Page 241).

While you certainly want to sell them more products, and get referrals, you need to make sure that any changes that occur within the account have been addressed or evaluated.

Speaking of getting referrals, make sure that you ask your contact about specific groups, like other decision-makers in different departments within her company, or friends in any associations that she belongs to. If you specify a type of contact, like members of a club or an association, you will help her focus on the faces of those people.

While resolving problems is a good thing, you might be interested in a way to turn that problem into a positive event. Read on.

*   *   *

CHAPTER 6: Keeping the Flame Alive

TOPIC 6.3: Spin Control

SKILLSET TOPIC(s)
❏   Problem Conversion

OBJECTIVE
To review ideas to resolve problems and potentially benefit from them instead of letting problems derail your account.

BENEFITS
✓   Resolve problems rapidly and efficiently.
✓   Increase sales by turning a problem into a positive.
✓   Reduce customer churn.
✓   Block your competitors' advances.

> "When you dodge your customer's calls, you leave that account extremely vulnerable to your competitors, who are much more likely to get an appointment while your client is feeling unloved."

Regardless of which profession you are in, bad things sometimes happen. On those rare occasions when something major does go wrong, you can take a page from the specialists who deal with damage control in the political arena.

They usually have catchy titles, like Public Relations Agents, Media Consultants, or Image Consultants, and they advise politicians on ways to minimize any potential damage that might occur if the public found out about something they fouled up. In other words, they look for a way to present the negative information about how dumb some politician has acted in a

This is commonly referred to as "spin control," because they put a positive spin on the negative information. It is a technique that you should use when dealing with customer problems. Instead of reacting in a panic when a customer calls you to scream about some foul-up, whether it is your fault or the result of someone else dropping the ball, take a moment to consider how the damage could be minimized (controlled) or even turned to your advantage (spun).

Using this approach will usually give you new alternatives, instead of being stuck with repeating the typical response that we are all tempted to use, which is to dodge their phone calls in the hopes that the problems will just go away. The problem is that the customers will go away, unlike some of those dates that you wish you could forget.

Dodging a problem call is actually the worst thing that you could possibly do, because that just causes them to get even more upset than they already are, which will leave the account extremely vulnerable to competitors. Any salesperson who contacts that client is likely to get an appointment to present an alternative to him while he is feeling unloved.

You won't have to dodge his calls if you can provide solutions, which is easy to do with the samples on the enclosed disk. At the very least, you will be able to respond in a way that proves that you are trying to help if you follow the suggestions that we discussed for handling delivery problems (Page 203).

While the call from an irate customer will probably never become a pleasant part of your responsibilities, I believe that you can usually turn it into a positive if you take the time to think about it. Let me give you an example.

When I was a sales manager, I once received an irate call from a new client while their salesperson was on <u>his</u> honeymoon. As the client described the problems that they were having, it was evident that their billing had somehow gotten fouled up beyond belief. I apologized for his inconvenience, because he was really upset, asked a few reasonably intelligent questions, and promised to make inquiries. The solution required multiple phone calls to several people at corporate headquarters, after which I called the client back to give him an update, etc. Naturally, the problem was not solved by the next billing cycle, which resulted in another nasty call from the client.

By this time their account manager had returned from his honeymoon, but he was too worn out to handle the problem. Having already become involved (although I hate being the outside point of a love triangle), I took the call and explained the steps that I had taken. We agreed to go to separate corners of the ring to await the results of the next round of calls I would make, and the problem was resolved shortly thereafter.

It is my firm belief that our client would not have been as patient had I not originally called back to tell him that I had called corporate to fix the problem, and sent them a brief letter thanking him for his patience.

The positive results ended up being much greater than just keeping the account. Within a couple of months after the problem was resolved, we got another call from the same client. He referred another branch of their organization that signed up for even more pagers than the original account. My salesperson was ecstatic, I got a great bonus, and the client sent us a glowing testimonial letter. What could be better? Well . . .

Spin control goes one step further than damage control, turning a potentially negative circumstance into a positive factor that you can leverage for additional goodwill, and even generate more business.

The best example that I can remember of how a potentially negative situation was turned into a positive occurred when another major account executive sold a paging system with voice mail, to a very large company. In fact, the voice mail feature actually won the sale, because at that time it was considered high-tech.

Murphy's Law was in effect from the very beginning. The equipment arrived late at our office, some of the units didn't work when they were tested, and the salesperson, John, had a lot less hair by the time the order was finally ready to deliver. We had already rescheduled delivery once before, which usually does not impress a client.

On the same day the pagers were due to be delivered for the second time, our operations manager informed John that the disk storage capacity of the voice mail system had reached maximum capacity. As a result, we would not be able to activate their voice mail for at least a week, at which time the replacement drive was scheduled to arrive.

We went to the general manager and explained that we couldn't deliver the pagers without the voice mail, we couldn't delay the delivery again, and we were sure that the client would cancel the order unless some miracle occurred. After a lot of whining, he finally agreed to cut back the voice storage time of our internal units, which would allow us to give John's client limited voice mail capability. The operative word was "limited," which left John on the verge of a nervous breakdown.

When he returned from delivering the new account, John seemed to be very cheerful, so I asked him how it went. I had first put on a bulletproof vest, in case John had had a nervous breakdown. He explained that on the way to the client's office, he was considering various ways to end his life without depriving his wife of their life insurance benefits, but he thought of a good way to present the situation to the client.

John started out by telling the client that he was a victim of Murphy's Law, explaining how the drive had been maxed out, etc., but that he had pleaded and begged the general manager to intervene since he knew how important the voice mail feature was. When he explained that we were able to get his voicemail activated by cutting back on the storage capacity of all of our employees, the client was apparently quite flattered instead of being upset that he would only have 50% capacity for a week.

In my opinion, had John not taken the initiative to reorient his own attitude in order to present the problem positively to the client (he was understandably upset when he first left the office), we would undoubtedly have ended up with a dissatisfied customer. As it turned out, that client referred three other accounts to John, and as far as I know they are, themselves, still growing customers.

Anyway, back to my tale of woe. Of course the new drive did not arrive in time, and the problem got so bad that we had to cut all of our customer's voice mail storage capacity back by 20% for several days before the problem was finally resolved. Believe it or not, my sales team was actually able to turn even that potentially disastrous situation into a goodwill mission. They called every major client to explain what had happened to cause the temporary voice mail abbreviation BEFORE the customers started calling us to complain.

Although all they really did was apologize for the inconvenience, and promise as speedy a cure as possible, we didn't lose a single customer (although we did lose an employee when the salespeople killed the operations manager). We even introduced a new product to our client base with overwhelming success a few months later.

Please don't misunderstand my point. Our clients deserved no less than that proactive service call, and your clients also deserve to be treated with dignity. It is always nice, however, when you get an unexpected reward for doing your job.

Don't be afraid of finding problems, because you can often take advantage of them by using spin control to pick up some serious brownie points.

As an example, there are times when technicians have to turn off a paging system in order to work on it. They try to do that late at night, or on the weekend, but some people are still affected, like hospitals, doctors who are on call, towing companies, etc. If you sold pagers, shutting down the system could clearly be a problem, or it could be turned to your advantage. If you hide while the system is down, you might have some unhappy customers, but not if you called anyone who might be affected in advance. Even if they were not planning to use their beepers at that time, they would still be grateful for the thoughtfulness.

In conclusion, positive spin control is the art of looking at a negative situation with the objective of figuring out if there is any potential benefit, or at least a positive way of presenting the information, regardless of how negative it may first appear to be.

If you handle the problem situations effectively, you can build goodwill instead of losing the account. You may not be able to avoid getting bummed out when things go wrong, because that's just a natural reaction, but the trick is to avoid giving in to frustration and self-pity. Being creative can turn some of the unavoidable negative situations that occur into greater commissions and improved customer satisfaction.

Isn't it worth taking the time to think through a particular problem, to seek the potential positive spin, rather than to merely sulk about it? Complaining is easier, but far less profitable.

If you do a good job of spin control, you can even reap an additional reward. When a prospect asks you for customer references, you could really distinguish yourself from the rank-and-file salespeople competing with you by using some of those customers you have helped as a reference. That way, your prospect will know for sure that you intend to honor your vows to love and cherish until . . .

* * *

MODULE 6.3: Case Study

Scenario #1

Prospect: Association of the Romantically Deprived

Sometimes things go wrong while you are managing large accounts, even when you do everything right. As an example, around the time of contract renewal, you meet with Frank Lonelee to make sure that there are no outstanding problems that you need to address, and, sure enough, they have had problems receiving pages in a certain building, which you did not know.

When you leave his office, you run through your options. First, you will try to solve the problem. If you can't provide an alternative solution, then you will probably have to try explaining how the other advantages of your product/service more than make up for the minor inconvenience. If that doesn't work, the only solution will be prayer. Just in case, you will also go out and find a new customer to replace the Association.

In this case, after doing your homework, you find out that pagers on a different frequency will resolve the problem, so you take care of it. After you deliver the new pagers, you send a follow-up letter to Frank.

TRUEBEEP CORPORATION
The paging solutions company

December 28, 1999

Mr. Frank Lee Lonelee
Association of the Romantically Deprived
6200 Love Drive
Romance, Maryland 20000

Dear Frank:

As always, I enjoyed having the opportunity to meet with you recently. The problem you have experienced with your crew assigned to the Pyramid Building will be resolved by using a different frequency for their pagers, one that will penetrate the subbasement environment.

Your account is important to us, and we will continue to do everything in our power to make sure that you receive the best support possible.

The other issues that we discussed will be addressed at our next meeting, scheduled for January 13, at 1:00 p.m.

Please call me if I can be of further assistance at (301) 555-9999.

Sincerely,

Alan Salesperson
Association Paging Service Specialist

AS/twp
Enclosure

Not too long afterwards, at a quarterly review meeting, you find out that the geographic coverage needs of some of the Association's staff has changed, and you do some homework to see if you can change their service to satisfy their new needs. After that meeting you send the following letter:

TRUEBEEP CORPORATION
The paging solutions company

January 14, 2000

Mr. Frank Lee Lonelee
Association of the Romantically Deprived
6200 Love Drive
Romance, Maryland 20000

Dear Frank:

Thank you for giving Truebeep the opportunity to continue to support your paging needs. As a valued customer, we look forward to helping you now, and in the future.

As a means of solving the problem that you have experienced with coverage for your new territories, we are happy to be able to offer you expanded coverage. This is a new system that we only recently completed, which operates on a 900 Megahertz frequency to give you the best range and penetration for your employees, to ensure that they receive all of their pages.

Your current rate of $XX.00 per pager will be maintained, and all of your current pagers will be exchanged for new pagers at no charge. Should you have any further questions, please contact me at (301) 555-9999.

Sincerely,

Alan Salesperson
Association Paging Services Specialist

After a relatively trouble-free period, Murphy comes back for a visit. You receive a lot of calls from various clients who have had a lot of difficulty getting through to your terminal. Apparently the telephone lines keep getting overloaded, so they end up getting a busy signal. Your engineers figure out that there are not enough telephone lines to support the traffic flow and order additional lines. You send the following letter.

TRUEBEEP CORPORATION
The paging solutions company

March 21, 2000

Mr. Frank Lee Lonelee
Association of the Romantically Deprived
6200 Love Drive
Romance, Maryland 20000

Dear Frank:

I would like to take this opportunity to confirm the information that we recently discussed. The billing for your account will be credited for the month of February due to our system problem of busy-outs. This inconvenience has been resolved as of March 1, when we doubled the number of telephone lines available to our customers.

Truebeep has made a commitment to our customers to maintain the highest level of customer service in the paging industry. We apologize for the inconvenience, and will ensure that this type of problem is avoided by being more proactive in terms of our system maintenance in the future.

Please contact me if I can be of assistance prior to our next meeting. My local pager number is 555-5555 for Baltimore and 888-8888 for Virginia and Washington, DC.

Sincerely,

Alan Salesperson
Association Paging Services Specialist

100 Beep Boulevard . Pageheaven . Maryland . 20003 . (301) 999-6666

Regardless of what problem you have to resolve for a client, explain it by phone or mail. While your call or letter might not make up for the inconvenience, dodging their calls and ignoring them completely is guaranteed not to result in additional business from that client.

Again, if the inconvenience is significant, try to get some type of credit for the affected parties. If you try to get a credit before the client calls to ask for one, they will usually be satisfied with less, so you might even end up saving your company some money.

You finally get promoted to management, so you send Frank the following letter to transfer the account to your replacement and set an appointment to introduce his new account manager.

Sending a notification letter when there is a change like this has a lot of benefits. It can help you take control of an account that you inherit, or represent a professional way to help whoever takes over your accounts. The customer will appreciate the courtesy, and will do more business as a result.

In addition, when you are promoted or transferred, some of your larger pursuits will still be going through their internal approval process. If you transfer those active prospects, as well as your established customers, you will leave a very grateful constituency behind you.

Everyone will be singing your praises, and you can always count on the support of your replacement, as well as your former supervisor, and who knows when that might come in handy?

TRUEBEEP CORPORATION
The paging solutions company

May 2, 2000

Mr. Frank Lee Lonelee
Association of the Romantically Deprived
6200 Love Drive
Romance, Maryland 20000

Dear Frank:

I would like to confirm our meeting to introduce John Bigaccount, who will be your new account manager as a result of my recent promotion, scheduled for 2:00 PM on May 18.

Our intent is to maintain the same level of service to our larger accounts by ensuring that account transfers such as this are handled smoothly. As always, your new account manager will be assigned a limited number of clients. We are committed to maintaining the integrity of our customer service program as we grow.

I look forward to meeting with you, and feel confident that we can maintain the excellent level of service you have grown accustomed to. Please contact Mr. Bigaccount, your new account manager, at (301) 555-9999 if you have any questions, or need any assistance.

Sincerely,

Alan Salesperson
Sales Manager

AS/twp

TOPIC 6.3: Assignment

1) List some of the typical problems that you run into.

2) Develop form letters, etc. to cover them.

Disk: Assignment Folder

"Success requires hard work, but the rewards more than compensate. On the other hand, you could always put this book on the shelf because it is too much work, and tell stories about the big ones that got away."

If you take the time to use some of the tools that you have learned to spice up your sales technique, there is no limit to the income you can earn. You still can't buy permanent happiness, but you can be pretty happy when you have no worries. Of course, there is no free lunch.

In order to be very successful in selling to major accounts, you have to do your homework. You need to understand the profile, criteria, market anomalies, and the psychology of the buyer(s) to decide which steps to take in order to compete effectively for each targeted account. And you definitely need to continually shop your competition.

As an integral part of your total marketing strategy you first need to identify the significant opportunities in your market area based on traditional vertical markets that use a significant amount of your service.

In order to minimize wasted time, you should also call on prospects that surround targeted prospects and customers that you schedule appointments with. Once you find the individuals and organizations that are positioned to recommend and/or buy your products and services, they have to be qualified and classified. You also need to identify any significant factors that might extend their buying cycle, which would require multiple prospecting and sales calls.

As long as you ask the right questions, you will have enough information after your first date to decide whether to pursue a relationship, and how to proceed. It pays to set up a core list of basic questions that you need to know about every prospective account, and add additional questions for each specific industry.

At this point your database becomes increasingly important. Large accounts will require more support activity and more sales steps than small accounts. That is especially true when you start the sales process with large corporations well before their contracts expire. Using a calendar to keep track of a few leads would be easy, but as the results of your prospecting and the activity relating to each prospect accumulates, you will outgrow that system.

You need to have instant access to your leads and be able to tell what has already been done in order to figure out your next step and what results you should expect from each action. The solution is to use a coding system on your lead cards or computerized database so that you can keep track of your activity.

Your lead system will also provide you with a source of "warm" calls that you can mix in with your "cold" calls to total strangers. This will break up the monotony and become critical for generating new sales opportunities efficiently once you become really busy supporting and growing your accounts.

Once you decide to pursue a prospect, you need to develop a viable plan to choreograph the steps of the sale to match their probable delivery date. Your plan should be based on the strategy that you feel will provide you the greatest chance of winning the account, which is, in turn, based on the variables you face.

Your objective is to determine the necessary sales steps that you need to take at the optimum time so that when you make your offer, you will have provided your contact with more than enough information to feel comfortable choosing you, thereby making the decision a "No-brainer."

Even if you do not get a signed contract when you present your Offer Summary, you will have better than an 85% probability of getting it at the implementation meeting. Remember that if it would truly be in the best interests of your prospective client to select your service, you have an obligation to help them make the right decision. Asking for the order is thus a natural process of helping others achieve their objectives.

To avoid having to continue cold-calling forever, follow through with your customers as diligently after the agreement is signed as before. If you make sure the decision-maker(s) are happy with the implementation of your product/service and delirious about your follow-up, they will continue to do business with you, and will recommend you to others. That will guarantee you a respectable income as you make your way through the next century.

In conclusion, I am not saying that you won't sell some large accounts without going the extra mile, just that you will win a lot more if you do. It is all up to you.

The real question is . . .

How Badly Do You Need to Succeed?

*　　*　　*

APPENDIX

Exhibit A

Exercise Answer Keys

I have tried to provide specific answers to the different exercises in the keys that follow, but in some cases the answers to a particular exercise are based on the type of product/service that you sell, and the market that you are targeting. If my answers do not seem to correspond to yours, please review the related topic.

TOPIC 1.1

1. The purchasing dynamics that you might face are as follows:

VARIABLES	SIZE	
	SMALL	LARGE
CONTACT	Decision-maker	Recommender
VULNERABILITY	High	Low
COMPETITION	Moderate	Cut-throat
EVALUATION	Emotional	Spreadsheet
SALES CYCLE	1 - 6 weeks	4 - 52 weeks

2. The typical reasons that large organizations are difficult to sell to are:

Multiple layers of management

Multiple departments

Multiple locations

Check and balance approval process

Changes like restructuring, and acquisitions

Loyalty to incumbent vendor/fear of change

TOPIC 2.1

❑ · If you chose a particular vertical market because you have an edge in that arena, then you are right on the money. If not, you need to review other vertical markets until you identify one, or more, where you do have an advantage.

❑ As far as the qualities that you need to look for in a major account, they should include any variables that would indicate their potential of being a major user of your product/service, such as:

#Employees

Revenue

Annual sales

Multiple locations

Multiple divisions

Have Subsidiaries

Etc.

Topic 2.2

❑ The two marketing approaches discussed in this topic are:

a) **Shotgun Marketing:** Randomly calling or visiting any business that could qualify for your service, regardless of size.

b) **Target Marketing:** Selecting companies based on specific criteria, within vertical markets that historically have a need for a large volume of your product or service.

❑ Your answers to this question could consist of any combination of benefits, weaknesses, and sources from the lists that follow:

Advantages

Shotgun	Targeted
• Excellent territory penetration • Variety of business applications • Concentrated activity pattern • More appointments/less driving • Referrals to adjoining businesses • Large quantity of prospects • Short average sales cycle • Decisions are less price sensitive • Easier to penetrate • Less competitive • Deal directly with decision-maker	• Requires less qualifying • Large average volume orders • Less customers to manage • Industry specialization (you become an expert on their industry) • Reference selling • "Birds of a Feather" referrals

Weaknesses

Shotgun	Targeted
• Requires more qualifying • Less vertical market specialization • Smaller average account size • Larger customer base to manage • Referrals will typically be smaller accounts	• Small window of prospects • More competitive market • Wider geographic distribution • Longer buying cycle • Hard to penetrate • Require intense maintenance • Decisions are pricing sensitive • Seldom deal with decision-maker

Sources

Shotgun	Targeted
■ CHAMBER OF COMMERCE DIRECTORIES ■ TRADE ASSOCIATIONS ■ BUSINESS JOURNALS ■ TRADE JOURNALS ■ *CONTACTS INFLUENTIAL* ■ NEWSPAPERS ■ REFERRALS ■ PROSPECTING WHILE TRAVELING ■ COMPETITOR'S LISTS ■ LOST CUSTOMERS	■ THE INTERNET ■ NATIONAL BUSINESS LIST BROKERS, LIKE AMERICAN BUSINESS LISTS, AND DUN & BRADSTREET ■ *R.L. POLK & COMPANY CITY DIRECTORY* ■ *DUN & BRADSTREET MILLION DOLLAR DIRECTORY* ■ *MARTINDALE HUBBLE DIRECTORY* ■ MANUFACTURER DIRECTORIES ■ *AMERICAN MEDICAL DIRECTORY* ■ OTHER LIBRARY SOURCES

TOPIC 2.3

1. The list of buying centers for each of your vertical markets might be somewhat different, based on what they do, but most organizations have some or all of the following departments:

- Customer Service
- Engineering
- Field Service
- Information Services
- Installation
- Purchasing
- Maintenance
- Operations
- Sales
- Security
- Telecommunications

2. The key to effective prospecting is to make sure that you do schedule time for it, and then make every effort to stick to your schedule.

3. When other activities interfere, you should exchange the original prospecting time slot with the next time slot that you have scheduled for the activity that you had to perform instead of prospecting.

4. The best time to organize your leads is during those hours that you would be unable to talk to prospects and customers.

TOPIC 3.1

❑ Congratulations to you if the questions that you came up with are close to the ones listed (as they would relate to your particular product/service). If not, it should make more sense after you complete the assignment for Topic 3.1, based on one of your own prospects.

ADDITIONAL INFORMATION NEEDED

Q *Do they have any coverage problems with either pagers or cellular?*

A They do have coverage problems with pagers in several buildings.

Q *What is the average hourly cost of the field service staff?*

A The average hourly cost of field service staff is $40.

Q *How much time is lost finding phone jack, dialing in?*

A Service staff waste an average of 15 minutes two times per day finding a phone jack to dial in.

Q *How much do they bill per hour?*

A The average hourly billing rate is $150 (you are considering a career change).

Q *What would it cost if they lost a client?*

A They bill an established client an average of $80,000 per year for maintenance and upgrades.

Q *Are there any other communications problems?*

A In addition to customer response problems, the technicians do not always get all of the information that they need when they are paged, so they have to call in. The call-in may take from 5 to 10 minutes, especially if the person they are calling isn't at their desk. It happens at least once a day.

Q *What are other departments, how many pagers/cell phones?*

A The sales group has 150 pagers/cell phones.

TOPIC 3.2

STEP #2

PROFILE

PROJECT: NetCom
BUYING CYCLE: 5 months for primary, 11 months for secondary
SALES CYCLE: 5 - 8 sales calls
ACCOUNT VOLUME: Very Large

OBJECTIVES	Resolve John's fear of new technology by stressing the technical capabilities of your system, and by getting substantial references from companies in his industry.
STRATEGY	Put together a more detailed technical package for the proposal, with particular attention to the system backup measures (get together with your system engineer).
	Get the names of several references from the other salespeople (bring it up at the next sales meeting, might also want to check to see if there is anything special that they did for their customers).
	Get John to field test the unit at least 30 days before they begin contract review, so that he has confidence in the coverage and capabilities. You need to help him set up the testing criteria, because the last time a prospect did the test they didn't set any parameters, so no-one really knew if the test was a success.
	Set up a meeting with NetCom's installation and support team leaders to get more specific details about the communication problems they are having, and the impact on productivity. Probably a good idea to have John there, so he knows that it is not just your version.
CLASSIFICATION	You have 4 months before the decision will be made, and another month to organize delivery, but you need to set up the field test within 30 days, because they begin contract review 90 days before contract expiration.
PROGNOSIS	Definitely worth pursuing, but there are still too many unresolved issues to forecast this one as a probable sale, so you are just going to mention it to your sales manager as a possibility.

STEP #3

Your Action Plan

ACTION	DATE
■ Develop the criteria for a field test.	
■ Set up a field test (to begin within 30 days).	
■ Contact the sales VP to find out about their units – same contract?	
■ Check with others at sales meeting for references and special applications.	
■ Check with chuck to verify your system back-up (is it any better that SlowBeep & AllCall systems?).	
■ Verify references.	
■ Call John to set up meeting with the installation and support team leaders.	
■ Beef up the technical package for the proposal, and develop a Return on Investment analysis that focuses on the value of time saved, so that you can offset the higher cost of your system.	
■ Develop proposal/present.	
■ Schedule facility walk-through.	
■ Conduct Implementation meeting/deliver.	

Possible Alternative Actions:
- ❏ Identify other departments that use pagers
- ❏ Talk other departments into using pagers
- ❏ Replace some of the highest cellular users

TOPIC 4.2

❑ The following sections of a formal proposal should always be customized, although some of the other sections will also have to be changed occasionally, as in the NetCom example, where you needed to beef up the technical information that you supplied to overcome a fear of new technology.

Specifications
_____

Recommendations
_____

Pricing
_____

References
_____

TOPIC 4.4

NETCOM ROI CALCULATION

A) LABOR COST SAVINGS

Labor Cost

Employee hourly pay	=	$40.00
internal cost (22% x $40.00)	=	$ 8.80
(for taxes, benefits, & holidays)		
TOTAL HOURLY COST	=	$48.80

Savings Calculation (Annual):

50 employees x $24.40 savings per hour	=	$ 1,220 per hour
X 8 hours savings per employee/month	=	$ 9,760 per month
3 year contract = $ 9,760 mo x 36 months =		$351,360 total savings

B) INCREASED BILLING POTENTIAL

Calculation (Annual):

50 employees x $24.40 savings per hour	=	$ 1,220 per hour
X 8 hours savings per employee/month	=	$ 9,760 per month
3 year contract = $ 9,760 mo x 36 months =		$351,360 total savings

TOPIC 5.2

1) You need to address the following account management areas with most major accounts:

Account management strategy
_____

Billing procedures
_____

User list/directory
_____

Account management reports
_____

2) A typical Account Support Guide would contain the following sections:

INITIAL:

Investigation notes
_____

Proposal
_____

Agreement
_____

Memos generated by client
_____

User Directory
_____

Account management/billing issues
_____

Quarterly account review schedule
_____

FUTURE:

Exception reports
_____

Quarterly review agenda
_____

Quarterly review minutes
_____

Optional product/services available
_____

EXHIBIT B

DISK DIRECTORY

📁 **ACCOUNT SUPPORT GUIDE** (Samples)
- ✓ Cover
- ✓ Implementation
- ✓ Issues
- ✓ Directory
- ✓ Agenda
- ✓ Minutes
- ✓ Review

📁 **ASSIGNMENTS**
Correspond to the examples at the end of the topic, keep original file for repeat use.

📁 **EXERCISES**
Correspond to the examples at the end of the topics.

📁 **LETTERS** (Samples)
- ✓ Response to Inquiry
- ✓ Cold Solicitation
- ✓ Referral
- ✓ Appointment Confirmation
- ✓ Follow-up – First Meeting
- ✓ Savings Analysis
- ✓ Group Rate Offer
- ✓ Follow-up – Delivery
- ✓ Account Credit – Problem Resolution

📁 **PROPOSAL**
Complete document that you can customize as needed for the different applications that you run into.

📁 **SIC LISTING**

📁 **STRATEGY/ACTION PLAN**
Blank forms to work out a strategy and action plan for new prospects, keep original file.

Exhibit C

Basic Tutorial

I have written this tutorial for those who are not very experienced in using Microsoft Word, so the steps are extremely basic. If anything seems confusing, refer to the Help directory. If you are already an experienced user, you can obviously use shortcuts where appropriate. Bill Gates clearly has nothing to fear from me.

Step 1: Insert disc into A drive

Step 2: Click on A drive to open files

Step 3: Double-click on the folder that you want to open

Step 4: Double-click on the file that you want to open

Step 5: Before working on a file, complete the following steps to save the original.
- ✓ Move your cursor to the top command bar and click on File.
- ✓ Click on Save As
- ✓ Click on File Name
- ✓ Add 1 at end of file name (preceding the period)
- ✓ Click on Save
- ✓ Start working on the file

Step 6: To save the file you are working on:
- ✓ Move your cursor to the top command bar and click on File.
- ✓ Click on Save

Step 7: To change a document, like a letter, form, or proposal section, complete the following steps:

A) Typing the change
- ✓ Move your cursor to the beginning of the section that you want to change
- ✓ Highlight that section
- ✓ Begin typing
- ✓ Repeat Step 6 to save changes

B) Inserting the change
- ✓ Open the file from which you want to insert
- ✓ Highlight the section you want to insert
- ✓ Move your cursor to the top command bar and click on Edit.
- ✓ Click on Copy
- ✓ Click on File, (top bar)
- ✓ Click on close
- ✓ Click on File
- ✓ Click on close
- ✓ Click on File
- ✓ Click on Open
- ✓ Click on arrow next to Look In window
- ✓ Click on floppy (A)
- ✓ Double click on the folder you want to open
- ✓ Double click on the file you want to open
- ✓ Move your cursor to the beginning of the section that you want to change
- ✓ Highlight that section
- ✓ Move your cursor to the top command bar and click on Edit.
- ✓ Click on Paste
- ✓ Repeat step 6 to save the changes

EXHIBIT D

SHOTGUN RESEARCH SOURCES

❑ **CHAMBER OF COMMERCE DIRECTORIES:** Most Chambers of Commerce compile various lists and directories of member companies. The information available will vary from Chamber to Chamber, so you need to call your local Chamber office for details.

❑ **TRADE ASSOCIATIONS:** Many trades and businesses maintain local, regional, and national associations, like the Home Builder's Association, Associated General Contractors, Independent Insurance Agent's Association, and Realtor Associations, for which membership lists may be available.

❑ **BUSINESS JOURNALS:** In virtually every city, there is a weekly or monthly local business publication or magazine, generally available at newsstands or bookstores, in which there are articles and advertising which may result in leads.

❑ **TRADE JOURNALS:** These are different from Business Journals in that the articles and advertising will relate to one trade or business rather than general business in a geographic area. You can find these magazines in the offices of prospects and customers, and should check them out while you are waiting for the prospect.

❑ *CONTACTS INFLUENTIAL*: *Contacts Influential* is a listing of businesses and individuals which many companies subscribe to, where you can order specific lead groups. This can work just as well for Shotgun marketing as for Target marketing.

❑ **NEWSPAPER SOURCES:** There are a multitude of potential prospect sources available in newspapers, i.e., business-to-business classifieds, since help wanted ads are a good source to find out which companies are adding sales or service staff. In many states it is required that you advertise that you are beginning a new business. These are generally near the classified section. Normal display advertising, especially in the business section, and specials such as landscape, real estate, and home repair, can also provide sources of new business.

❑ **REFERRALS**: This is actually the most potent source of qualified leads, and often the least well-used. Every contact you make should include a request for referrals. In addition to new sales from existing customers, you should ask for referrals every time you make a prospecting call, even if the prospect refused to make an appointment. This may sound weird, but a prospect who turned you down may just feel a bit guilty and want to help you.

❑ **PROSPECTING WHILE TRAVELING**: Every day you see new businesses opening up, new vehicles being delivered to a business, businesses relocating to larger quarters, and delivery trucks (with names and telephone numbers on the side). Invest in a small tape recorder to record this information for daily review. That information could help you find the right approach to get an appointment. For example, if a company is in the middle of moving, they would probably be more susceptible to a precall letter than an unscheduled visit (while they are dealing with various moving disasters).

❑ **COMPETITOR LISTS**: Most salespeople give their prospects lists of accounts as references. When you win a new account, your contact may let you review the competitive bids (with reference list).

❑ **LOST CUSTOMERS**: Many companies generate a report that lists lost customers. Those customers are well worth a follow-up call. If they signed a new agreement with someone else, say for one year, you should call a few times over the year and increase the frequency of contact in the last three months. Find out why they left, because, hopefully, conditions will have changed in your company. It would be even better if your competitor has dropped the ball.

TARGETED RESEARCH SOURCES

❑   **THE INTERNET:** The information highway is by far the easiest and most comprehensive source of information on the planet today. If you already surf the Net, you know that it is a great way of getting information about companies that have Web sites. If you are not using the Internet for research, you are missing a truly amazing resource.

Looking at a prospect's site can tell what they do, how they do it, what is important to them, and who their customers are. In addition to being knowledgeable about their business, which is important, you can also draw conclusions that could impact your strategy.

For instance, if a company's Web site is ultra high-tech, they will probably be receptive to new technology, whereas if it is extremely conservative they might be more receptive to the issue of the return on their investment. You can also find out who their competitors are, and what they are doing. That can aid you in making the sale, and serve as part of your vertical market strategy.

Unfortunately, not every company has a Web site, so you will still need to use other sources for information.

❑   **NATIONAL BUSINESS LIST BROKERS:** Organizations like American Business Lists, and Dun & Bradstreet offer cards or computerized lists for private sale, and American Business List's CD is available in the library. The information listed includes business name, contact, type of business and telephone number, and can be ordered according to very specific criteria, like industry, number of employees, annual sales, type of organization (like national or local, etc.), or by geographic preference.

❑   ***R.L. POLK & COMPANY CITY DIRECTORY:*** This, or a similar directory, can be found in virtually any library. The directory contains alphabetical lists of every business in the trade area, and a street-by-street list of every individual and business in the city. Information about individuals includes occupations, employer, and telephone number. Information about companies includes owners' or managers' names and telephone numbers.

❑   ***DUN & BRADSTREET MILLION DOLLAR DIRECTORY:*** This is a directory of businesses with more than one million dollars annual sales. There are several volumes to this directory, including alphabetical listings, geographical listings, and businesses by SIC code. Information about the businesses listed includes products produced, company officers, address, and telephone number.

☐ *MARTINDALE HUBBLE DIRECTORY*: A directory of lawyers and law firms listed by state. Information listed includes names, addresses, telephone numbers, and specialty.

☐ **MANUFACTURER DIRECTORIES**: Published by various companies and individuals, these directories are available in most public libraries. Businesses are generally listed alphabetically, geographically, and by SIC code. Information listed includes company name, owner or manager, type of business, number of employees, sales, and telephone number.

☐ *AMERICAN MEDICAL DIRECTORY*: Listed geographically, this directory contains virtually every doctor in an area, including name, address, and specialty.

☐ **ALTERNATE LIBRARY SOURCES**: There are numerous other directories available in the business and general reference sections of virtually every library, so I usually ask the reference librarian for assistance.

Corporate
Training
Specialists

"Taking sales performance to the next level."

MAXIMIZE YOUR TIME

Improve sales productivity with our sales training programs/products.
We can customize a program for your specific needs.

TRAINING PRESENTATION MODULES

Tired of covering the same information at your sales meetings or training sessions? Our materials will help you spice up your meetings, and dramatically improve sales productivity. You select only the skill module(s) that would most benefit your team, like prospecting, or developing a winning sales strategy.

Each module includes:

- ✓ Instructor's guide
- ✓ Multimedia or overhead presentation
- ✓ Hand-outs
- ✓ Exercises
- ✓ Report forms
- ✓ Tools to apply to prospects/clients
- ✓ Assignment(s)

SEMINARS

Get the advanced skills necessary to blow away sales quotas in just one day of intense interactive training with one of our certified trainers. Visit our web site at **www.corp-train.com** to get specific information about regional tour schedules for our personal or corporate training seminars.

WORKSHOPS

Give your sales team the tools they need to be successful in today's competitive environment with our two- or three-day customized workshop.

**For more information visit our web site at www.corp-train.com
or you can contact us at (888) 709-7676.**